OBSCENITY, ANARCHY, REALITY

OBSCENITY, ANARCHY, REALITY

CRISPIN SARTWELL

STATE UNIVERSITY OF NEW YORK PRESS

Cover photo by Richard Pospisil, Jr. 1995

Published by
State University of New York Press, Albany

For information, address State University of New York Press,
State University Plaza, Albany, N.Y. 12246

Production by M. R. Mulholland
Marketing by Dana E. Yanulavich

Library of Congress Cataloging-in-Publication Data

Sartwell, Crispin, 1958-
    Obscenity, anarchy, reality / Crispin Sartwell.
       p.   cm.
    Includes bibliographical references.
    ISBN 0-7914-2907-5 (hardcover : alk. paper). — ISBN 0-7914-2908-3
(pbk. : alk. paper)
    1. Conduct of life. 2. Sartwell, Crispin, 1958-   . I. Title.
BJ1581.2.S243 1996
128—dc20
                                    95-406
                                     CIP

10 9 8 7 6 5 4 3 2 1

THIS BOOK IS FOR
JUDITH BRADFORD,
WHO, AFTER IT WAS WRITTEN,
MADE IT REAL.

———————————

CONTENTS

INTRODUCTION

This book is about reality. It's about reality as the location of and as a way of living; it's about living in, and living as, reality. Finally, it's about loving the real: What I struggle toward in this book is the affirmation of what is, precisely as it is. This book explores what might happen if one were to eschew all efforts at the transformation of reality, except the effort to transform oneself into a person who is capable of loving the world. That position is, of course, itself inconsistent. To say of myself that I do not love the world sufficiently is to say that I ought to be transformed, and I, after all, am real: I am part of that which I am learning to love. Perhaps, then, I ought to affirm even this: that I cannot affirm the world unconditionally. But to say that I *ought* to do even that is incompatible with the affirmation of what is, precisely as it is.

In a true affirmation of the world, there could be no more "ought"s. For, as I will claim, to say that something ought to be the case is to consign what *is* the case to an imaginary oblivion. Every claim that something ought to be the case is a judgment that what is the case is insufficient. One might formulate the quandary this way: There ought to be no oughts. Thus, the notion of affirming the world is shattering; it transforms our values, or does not allow us any more values in the way values are traditionally understood. In Western philosophical history, ethics and aesthetics are the studies of what ought to be the case: every value that is valued in the Western philosophical tradition is incompatible with loving things as they are. Every value *demands* a transformation: we ought to be better than we are, or, more often, *you* ought to be better than *you* are;

that is, you ought not, as you are, to be. We cannot very easily conceive what would happen if we saw that all such attempts at transformation are pathological. Every flight from the world as it is expresses the pain inflicted by that world; all of our values are minted in fear and nurtured by cowardice. This book is, among other things, an attempt to find out what might happen to values in an affirmation of the world.

The results I arrive at will seem, I hope, disturbing. One project that is trashed in this book is the political state, which is problematic both on (anti)-ethical and (anti)-metaphysical grounds. I regard the state with ontological suspicion; I will suggest that the state, as it is usually understood, does not exist at all. And insofar as it does exist, the state is a grandiose project for the forcible transformation of what is. Every state is to that extent utopian: It dreams of a reality other than the one in which it is operating, even if that reality is merely one in which the dictator has become richer than he is. In that sense, the state is the codification or the fossilization of values; it is a machine for the forcible transformation of human beings. Fortunately, by that standard it is also a miserable failure.

In the course of developing post-ethical values that are compatible with loving life and loving the world, I explore the notions of obscenity and transgression. Because every moral assertion asserts that something ought to be the case—that is, that the world as it is presently constituted ought not to be the case—seduction into evil is an allowance of things to be. In this sense, violation of moral strictures may be a sacrament. The characteristic transgressions in Western culture are all affirmations of embodiment: Every obscene word is a reminder of the body, just as the fundamental religious disciplines of the culture arise in the pitiful effort of the disciple to transcend his body. Anything that reminds us that we are mammals scurrying around on the surface of a planet is thus worthwhile. Fucking is worthwhile, and also saying "fuck."

The term 'reality,' which I chant like a mantra throughout this book, is liable to give the reader pause. It has been used, for example, to pick out Plato's Ideas, or Brahman, or the atoms: It is always whatever underlies mere appearances; it has often enough been used to call us out of our everyday experience into some supposed other realm of the really real. All such uses of the term are inversions. Plato's Ideas are, precisely, unreal: the realm to which Socrates hoped to retreat, by dying out of the world. This book does not give any (well, it does not give many) arguments in ontology. In fact, I shall give reasons to regard ontology as pernicious, and try to avoid any ontological systematization. But what I mean by "reality" is the stuff we encounter every day in the world: trees, cars, the sky, buildings, earth, human beings. Any call to transcend such things into the really real ought to be regarded with the utmost suspicion. First of all, such things cannot be transcended except in an illusion: A human being always lives, while she lives, as situated within those things, as one of them and one with them. If you don't think cars are real, go out and let one pass through your body, especially if you don't think your body is real either. The fact is, you believe in the reality of cars, and so do I, and so does everyone who can live in this world.

To say that we are real is, finally, to say that there is no deep distinction between appearance and reality, though people undergo various piecemeal delusions. But saying that *this world* is a delusory appearance, whether its ultimate reality is described in terms of Ideas or itsy bitsy wavicles, is a symptom of how much we suspect ourselves. A glowing health, a real affirmation, would say, As things appear to me, so they are. I think well enough of myself to see that I am not a weaver of delusions but a true mirror and microcosm of the world.

Now, though I will not present an ontology here, I should say that I am suspicious of any purported object that we can't get our hands on and throttle properly. And the belief that *we* are not things of the sort that cars and trees are (that we are souls, for example, or that consciousness distinguishes us in or from the order of nature) is the philosophical expression of a self-loathing so deep and so entire that it must deny what is obviously the case, a self-loathing so intense and so thorough that it seeks to expunge every scrap of the self that is loathed. It is a form of suicide: We hate that we are bodies so much that we simply jettison our bodies imaginatively. If there were a God, the self-loathing of creatures such as we would be loathsome in his sight; health is always an acknowledgment of embodiment.

I am not going to argue for any of this, but I am going to try to show you that you already believe that this world is as real as anything can be. That is why the real is a shock, or why the experience of shock is important: because it brings us back to the real and, thus, to ourselves. Persons who are in intense pain, and who allow themselves fully to experience that pain, can doubt neither the reality of that pain's source nor the reality of themselves. Pain motivates flight, and intense, prolonged pain motivates, finally, a flight from the world. But as long as one can stick with one's pain, can hang in and allow oneself to be in pain, for that long no ontology is required. To be in pain is to live a demonstration of reality; it is to be forced toward reality. Pain is something that must be affirmed, and, of course, it is also the hardest thing to affirm. Pain is a call into the reality of what is real, and thus is something creatures such as ourselves radically require.

Thus, much of the history of philosophy and of religion is, in my view, pathological. Much of it is a flight, an obvious flight, from what is, just as the life of the scholar or priest or moralist is a long flight from the real world. This is a diagnosis that I owe to Nietzsche, and if there is a hero of this book, it is he. I read Nietzsche as a radical realist, and I will try to show why, though I depart from him completely when it comes to questions about power. I regard power as it is conceived within the Western tradition, power over the self and over others, as pernicious and delusory; when power expresses itself as the forcible attempt to remake people and circumstances, it is simply the expression of "values," the enactment of the assertion that what is ought not to be. But Nietzsche comes as close as the history of Western philosophy has yet progressed toward the affirmation of reality.

For as long as philosophy and religion have fled the world, for just so long have they returned again and again to it. I will try, in what follows, to concentrate on those figures who have mustered an affirmation, figures such as Chuang Tzu, the Tantric masters, Emerson, Black Elk, Bataille, and Vaclav Havel. The message of such figures is one of tremendous hope: hope that we can overcome our self-loathing and our loathing for the earth. Their message, finally, though delivered like a series of blows, is a message of love. When one asks a Zen master a conceptual question—such as, say, "What is the inmost nature of reality?"—the Zen master does not reply with a theory. Instead, he boxes your ears. This means two things. First, don't ask. And second, *this* is the inmost nature of reality; reality is what boxes you on the ears. The delusion, the snare, is to look beyond this, to look toward the inmost kernel. The outer husk *is* the inmost kernel; the appearance is the reality. You yourself are real, are "the ultimate nature of reality," though you must be cuffed on the ears to be reminded of what you already know. Spiritual discipline is an ever-greater embeddedness in the world; spiritual transcendence is only achieved in total immanence. There is no way out, no way around. Escape, evasion, denial—all, finally, are impossible. That you are real, that you are here, that this place, too, is real—that is enlightenment. In the words of the philosopher Joseph Diffie: "I want to go to heaven, but I don't want to go tonight." Right at this moment, I am content to be where I am and what I am: a human being living on the earth. Any philosophy that calls me elsewhere or calls me something else calls me also toward my own destruction and to the destruction of the earth.

Finally, what I seek from learning to love the world is an exhilaration, a dance that learns and loves even in the face of evil or that learns and loves even evil. I seek a way to orient myself physically into the world, a way to open myself in a gesture of welcome to all that is. I seek a joy that is incompatible with comprehension—incompatible, finally, with systems, concepts, answers, philosophies— that opens always on to the particular situation. Human beings are separated from the world not by the "veil of ideas" or by the mediation of language, not because they are souls or minds inexplicably entangled in a world of physical objects, and so forth, but because they hate themselves for being of the world, and hate the world for being. If this hatred were slowly to dissipate as we opened ourselves to the world, we might know an authentic love. It is into that love that I open this book.

1

THE SHOCK OF THE REAL

George Santayana once said that the experience of shock establishes realism.[1] That is a simple and profound observation. What it means is this: When you are shocked—when, say, you drop a bowling ball on your foot—it is not up to you whether to believe that the bowling ball and the foot are real. In the experience of shock, you are called into the reality of the world by your radical vulnerability to it. Like it or not, unless you are comatose or psychotic, at such moments you experience, accede to, and howl at the real. At such moments, and in virtue of such moments, you know the reality of the real, and know yourself to be real within it. Pleasure is forgetful; it lulls one toward sleep and toward self-congratulation. One can "forget oneself" in pleasure and even forget the source of the pleasure; one can enjoy the immersion and forget its origin. But pain and surprise bring with them a preternatural alertness, and alertness is an openness to what is.

Reality is impertinent, indefatigable, and inescapable. But reality is a source of pain, pain that sometimes cannot be tolerated. The history of Western thought and culture could be written as the history of attempts to deny, escape from, negate, control, or destroy reality and, in fitful oscillation, to affirm, accept, embrace, or love it. The first is cowardice, though perhaps absolutely necessary cowardice. It encompasses the profound, paltry, and pathological history of idealism, and inhabits like a parasite the philosophies of Plato and Hegel, Buddha and Shankara, Augustine and Descartes. As do many forms of cowardice, it issues in prodigies of pride and arrogance—for example, the claim that human beings construct the world, as formulated by Kant. Space and time are merely the forms of human perception: That assertion is a monstrosity of hubris.

On the other hand, the affirmation of the real is unutterably difficult. Allowing what is real to be is much harder for us than avoidance, denial, destruction, re-creation. For each of us, there are events, people, institutions we would like to reform or revise or expunge. But there is hope in affirmation, because reality, after all, is real. One may be able to evade this or that fact for a time; one may be able alter this or that circumstance. But to take up the annihilation or revision of reality as a whole, to take up the annihilation or revision of reality as one's fundamental posture within the real, is pitiable and hopeless. It is pitiable because it is a display of weakness; it is the expression of the fact that one has been crushed by the real, brought to one's knees. And it is hopeless because evasion, finally, is impossible; each of us is situated wholly within the real; each of us is, in fact, the real under one of its permutations, at one of its locations. Evasion of the real would entail, among other absurdities, evasion of ourselves. Every attempt to evade reality that does not issue in self-annihilation increases the pain and anger one feels at one's total immersion in what one finds intolerable.

I.

Descartes notoriously got modern philosophy going by doubting the existence of the external world. He wanted it proved that he was not dreaming, that an evil demon was not deceiving him, and so forth. Like Descartes, Santayana descends into scepticism, and he descends even more deeply that did Descartes: into the abyss of absolute ignorance about concepts, the world, and himself. For both thinkers, there is then a turning back into knowledge. The ascent begins for Descartes with the identification of a single certainty: Whether or not he is dreaming, Descartes knows that he himself exists. He then proceeds to demonstrate the existence of God, from which he demonstrates, finally, the existence of the world he perceives.

Descartes, then, mounts a demonstration of the falsity of scepticism about the external world. Santayana mounts no such demonstration—or rather, he mounts a demonstration in the sense of a gesture, a pointing, rather than in the sense of an argument. For Santayana, *shock* is the destruction of scepticism about oneself and the world. If you need to be convinced of the reality of the things you experience, don't read an argument; drop a bowling ball on your foot. Santayana writes:

> In brute experience, or shock, I have not only a clear indication, for my ulterior reflection, that I exist, but a most imperious summons at that very moment to *believe* in my existence. . . . Experience, even conceived most critically as a series of shocks overtaking one another and retained in memory, involves a world of independent existences deployed in an existing medium. Belief in experience is belief in nature. (*Scepticism and Animal Faith*, 142, 143)

The experiences, as Santayana puts it, of "utter blankness, intolerable strain, shrieking despair," (140) call us to and out of ourselves as and into what is real. They establish the existence of nature for us in the most compelling way such a thing could be established for beings such as we: animals rather than pure minds. The world denier almost always starts on himself, and what he says of himself is, first of all, that he is no animal or is an anomalous animal, that he is spirit, mind, and so forth; that he resides properly in heaven, or surveys evolution from the heights, as its crowning achievement.

Thus does world negation comport perfectly well with the "scientific" consciousness, as it does in other ways as well. Consciousness, it may be said, distinguishes us from or even in the order of nature. Our reason distinguishes us from the apes. The difficulty of believing such things as one actually goes through the day eating, shitting, sleeping, and fucking is a tribute to the power of the need for evasion that informs such views. Cowardice in the face of reality runs so deep that it leads one to ignore the most obvious facts about oneself.

I have heard it said that science "establishes," for example, that physical objects such as a table are not solid but consist mostly of empty space. Science tells us "the way things really are," and "the way things really are" is more or less completely distinct from the way things appear. This is a permutation of the old "spiritual" impulse to escape the real (this table, for instance) by recourse to the Real. The Real used to be thought of as the realm of Forms, Brahman, the Absolute, the Mind of God, and so forth. Now it is conceived as the "scientific image" behind the "manifest image." In either case, the experienced world is left behind. Thus, the things we experience every day are reduced to the status of "images," "pictures," as they are, also, for idealism and, for that matter, classical empiricism, logical positivism, and so on.

Now, it is worth asking why people *need* to reduce things to images. And there is an obvious answer: Images are *safe*. In my fantasy, in the world of images, I can commit horrific crimes and remain innocent. I can plunge off cliffs and awaken before I hit bottom. No one has ever been blown to bits by a picture of an explosion. So if the world as I experience it were an image, I would be perfectly safe. And the degree to which I *need* to treat the world as an image is the degree to which I feel *endangered* by the world and the degree to which I find all danger intolerable. But to treat the world I live in as a picture: that means there must be something of which it is a picture, a realm of the Really Real underlying the appearances. Nevertheless, this realm of the Really Real must be kept at arm's length, fended off, lest it, too, endanger us—thus Kant's "thing in itself" which underlies appearances but about which we can know absolutely nothing. The system is brilliant. But it reeks of fear and pain. That no one has ever been attacked by a quark is a good reason to use quarks in a fundamental ontology. But if I pick up this chair and slam it over your head, I wonder whether you can maintain your belief that it's not solid.

Corresponding to the notion that the world is a bunch of images or pictures is the notion that the human agent is a sort of moviegoer, beholding the world from the safety of her seat, or perhaps someone leafing through photo albums, embarrassed or pleased by the memories evoked by the photographs but beholding the represented experiences in safety. Representation, as it is conceptualized in the Western tradition, places the represented object at a distance, and this fact has been used, for example, to construct entire aesthetic systems (for example, Kant's, in which my pleasure before works of art is "disinterested," i.e., safe). To survey the world in representation is to feel an influx of security and power, as when one comprehends the world in an atlas. If we could conceptualize the world in its totality, *understand* it all, remove every suspicion of excess, shock, boundlessness, obscurity, we would have made ourselves safe. We can do this imaginatively by constructing fictions, or we can try to do it in fact by giving a "theory of everything" or by technologically controlling the environment. Science as a whole is an attempt to make us safe by comprehension.

It is an embarrassment for this view that the person enjoying the picture show can be punctured or crushed by her own pictures. But the view is maintained as a compensation for that vulnerability. The compensation is purely imaginary, but is nevertheless a compensation for all that. We read romance fiction, say, to "escape" for a bit, but we can also escape all day, every day, by turning our lives into romance fiction and our world into a fictional world where nothing bad ever happens and where, since bad things happen all the time, they happen only to fictional characters. Science, in that sense, can be used as romance fiction, just as can philosophy and religion and art.

"Science" could not possibly inform us that this table is not solid; we all know that the table is solid. "Science," in telling us that the table consists mostly of empty space, may be speaking the truth. But all this shows is that *what we mean by 'solidity'* has to be explained, finally, in a (somewhat, temporarily) surprising way. That is, solid objects consist mostly of empty space. This is an elucidation of what the world is like, as is, for example, the discovery that water is H_2O. That does not show water is not really wet, transparent, and so forth, just as showing that tables consist mostly of empty space does not show that they are not solid. Again: Nothing could possibly show this table not to be solid; we all know it to be solid. When science is used to elucidate the world as it appears, it is innocent enough. When it is used systematically to distinguish appearances from reality, it is a system of metaphysics and, in that sense, as false and as world-hating as any other system of metaphysics. And notice that science, just like aesthetics, "distances," that we are deimplicated in what we "study." Nietzsche puts it like this:

No doubt, those who are truthful in that audacious and ultimate sense that is presupposed by the faith in science *thus affirm another world* than the world of life, nature, and history; and insofar as they affirm this "other world"—look, must they not by the same token negate its counterpart, this world, *our* world?— But you will have gathered what I am driving at, namely, that it is still a *metaphysical faith* upon which our faith in science rests.[2]

The particular version of world-hatred typical of our century retreats into language: All experience, it says, is linguistically mediated or linguistically articulated. There are no "uninterpreted" facts, and interpretation is a linguistic activity, a sort of literary criticism (this is roughly the view, for example, of Hans-Georg Gadamer, Nelson Goodman, and Stanley Fish). The notion of narrative or, more widely, of text is central to recent philosophy. Figures such as Derrida, Rorty, and Richard Bernstein centralize text and story as "that in which we live and move."[3] (Here, Rorty is stating what he takes to be Derrida's view.) In particular, much recent work on race and gender describes narrative as the fundamental mode of social and personal constructions of self and world (Carolyn Heilbrun: "We are stories.") The hegemony of language in recent philosophy is in some ways subversive to the Western philosophical tradition. But in other ways it participates in and intensifies the most problematic aspects of that tradition. For example, in some of its overweening moments it elides the physical; it deemphasizes or textualizes the body.

It also makes scholarship of a certain sort a model for all human experience, and one of the things that drives the view is the same yearning for safety that drives idealism; I retreat from thing to interpretation in an attempt to gain control over things or to operate in a realm where I (or we) have some comfort (and, in the case of actual literary critics, some technique) and in which the poignancy and arbitrariness of things is attenuated.

The centralization of text and narrative challenges certain aspects of the political implications of Western metaphysics. When we perform a pseudoreduction of human experience or "the human world" to text, we may appear to be entangled precisely in a metaphysical system, a sort of parody of idealism. But notice that narratives are plural, equivocal, creative. "Textualism" can resist the "totalizing" or "master" narrative of Western metaphysics and rest content simply with the indefinite multiplication of texts. In this sense, textualism is more open, corrigible, and egalitarian than the metaphysical tradition. But it is also a view that reflects the centrality of texts to certain lives: the lives of the scholars who put forward the centrality of texts. It is not a view that would attract assembly-line workers, for instance. It is a projection of lives that *are* lived largely in and through texts onto human experience in general.

And let me issue a brief whine: The twentieth century in Western philosophy has been the era of language; we're hypnotized by language, trapped in language, obsessed by language, whether we're doing analytic theory of reference or ordinary language philosophy or deconstruction. Russell, Wittgenstein, Heidegger, Derrida—all of them participate in and intensify this obsession. The obsession had its uses, had its moments of exhilaration; it helped some. At this point, though, it's boring. If the next century is also a century obsessed by language, then I am going to catch up on some much-needed sleep. Let's see whether we cannot write about something other than writing, for a change. Reading this century's philosophy is like reading a tortured novel about a tortured novelist writing a tortured novel about a tortured novelist; it's self-indulgent, and it bloats the author's little sphere of activity into a world.

Nevertheless, and as advocates of the view are concerned to emphasize, people *can* be endangered by narratives and in narratives. One point of "textualism" is that texts have real effects; for example, people are *oppressed* by master narratives (or by those who formulate and impose them) associated with power. Narratives of race and gender seek to destroy the ability of African-Americans and women to tell their own stories or to possess their own language. Notice, however, that, if we were to make narrative central to power relations, we would be, to some extent, releasing power from its concrete physical manifestations. A policeman beating a suspect is endangering the suspect with his hands, not with his story. So, though narrative may have physical inscriptions and physical effects, the privileging of narrative performs an abstraction from material conditions.

At a minimum, narrative organizes or reconstructs human experience: There cannot be a narrative of everything, though what is omitted from a given narrative can, perhaps, in principle be taken up into *some* narrative. But narrative implies coherence. Though there can be diffuse and ambiguous narratives, there cannot be wholly random narratives; a collection of sentences does not count as a narrative unless it moves in a certain direction, displays a certain consistency and continuity. We need such things. The problem arises when we use the narrative to efface or expunge the random and the incoherent, which, in fact, explode moment by moment into our lives. To locate narrative as the central mode of human experience is to seek evasion of these intolerable aspects of the real. A letting-go into the incoherence that surrounds us would be a letting-go of narrative. That moment is as necessary as the construction of the narrative itself.

Considered as the stuff of narrative, my life sucks. I'm pretty good at constructing narratives, and perhaps I would like to convert my life into a story. But as a story, my life is boring and incoherent, an accumulation of details that, in five minutes, would beggar Proust. My life is long, excruciatingly long, and, finally, quite senseless. Every attempt I make to narrativize my life is radically impoverished in the face of the evident facts. If there is one thing that novels teach me, it is that my life is no novel and cannot even be described. If I am trying to construct a narrative of my life, I am trying to be something and somewhere other than I am. This confusion of the world with the description of the world, or rather, this attempt to replace the world with a description, lies at the heart of scientism as a metaphysics. Scientism, in this sense, seeks to replace what is elucidated with its elucidation, seeks a retreat to the safe realm of "knowledge," where knowledge is conceived linguistically. To describe something accurately is a beautiful and necessary activity. But to reduce things to descriptions is just a stupid mistake. And though "textualism" is multivocal where scientism is univocal, both detach us from the world behind a screen of descriptions.

We need meaning. But we (or, at any rate, I) need also to let go of meaning. It is possible to suffer from a lack of meaning but possible also to suffer from its surfeit. I will return to this theme at length, but, for now, let me just note that the drive for meaning can grow pathological, that meaning forecloses experience in certain ways. Narrative attenuates shock.

If I take the experience of shock seriously, and I *must*, when I experience it, then, as Santayana says, I will be led to "posit" not only a self but a certain sort of self, a self that is no spectator:

> Now that I am consenting to build further dogmas on the sentiment of shock, and to treat it, not as an essence groundlessly revealed to me, but as signifying something pertinent to the alarm or surprise with which it fills me, I must thicken and substantialise the self I believe in, recognising in it a nature that accepts or rejects events, a nature having a movement of its own, far deeper, more continuous and more biased than a discoursing mind: the self posited by the sense of shock is a living psyche. (*Scepticism and Animal Faith*, 147)

In short, the self posited in shock is not a story but an animal. What Santayana asks us to do is simply to acknowledge what we really do believe, to embrace an experience the reality of which we cannot deny except as an abstracted hypocrisy. For the interesting thing about narrative fiction is that it is flimsy, implausible; finally, a long-term immersion in it begins to soften the brain. But shock calls us forth from the romance we have so busily constructed around our lives. Shock shows us to be vulnerable to the world. To drop a bowling ball on one's foot is to know, to know beyond the possibility of doubt, that one is a physical body in contact with other physical bodies. Shock thus "wakes" us into the real, drags us out of our pictures, our narratives, in short, our reverie.

The reason that the experience of shock is more compelling than any argument is that it *demands* recognition that something is happening. From scholars, people who spend lives in a flight from what is really there, a flight to concepts and books and studies, acknowledgment of the reality of the real must be extorted. To drop a bowling ball on your foot is to realize what you knew quite well all along: that reality is opaque, dangerous, and out of your control. That is, to experience the real as real is to experience one's powerlessness before the real. This feeling of powerlessness is intolerable, or is often experienced as intolerable, and for that reason people would like to believe that the world is a fantasy, an image, a text, something that, finally, can be put under our control. I awaken from dreams; if I find one fantasy dissatisfying, I may be able to shift to another. I can put the book down, or reconstruct the narrative. But I cannot awaken from the world nor shift to another by an act of will or through social cooperation. To acknowledge the world's reality is to acknowledge my own limitations and to experience them. "Think how many rebuffs every man experiences in his day," writes Thoreau; "perhaps he has fallen into a horse-pond, eaten fresh-water clams or worn one shirt for a week without washing. Indeed, you cannot receive a shock unless you have an electric affinity to that which shocks you."[4] This "electric affinity" is what, in shock, shows us to be situated in the world, to be of the order of the real.

Physical pain, bereavement, sickness, a slow decline toward death—these are experiences we *need* in order to bring us back to reality and thus to ourselves. Not surprisingly, it is these very experiences which we seek to evade, vitiate, or disperse by the construction of, say, a philosophical system. To slap Georg Wilhelm Friedrich Hegel, for instance, would be to do him a signal service; it would be to call him out of the "world" as the Unfolding of the Absolute and into the world as the Attack of the Contingent. It would be to call him out of the general into the particular, out of the illusion of safety into the reality of danger, out of two-bit grandiose hypocrisy and into life. Of course, slapping someone is no argument. But I think all arguments here are perfectly trivial, whereas real openness to life is correspondingly profound.

II.

Much of the world's religious history is a pathological attempt to escape the world and to be other than human. But there are several conspicuous exceptions. The one I will discuss here is Zen. Zen Buddhism constitutes a discipline that forgoes every movement into the beyond, every movement outside the real. Zen monks perform the most menial tasks precisely as religious exercises, for in Zen there is no transcendence of the real, only deeper and deeper immersion. The Zen patriarch I-Hsuan (who lived in the ninth century and was also known as Lin-chi, which was the name of his monastery; he is called Rinzai by the Japanese) told his disciples, "All one has to do is move one's bowels, urinate, put on clothing, eat meals, and lie down when tired."[5] Enlightenment is to be found precisely where one already is, in the performance of one's animal functions. For an animal, allowing oneself to be an animal *is* enlightenment; it is an affirmation of reality.

The tenth-century Master Yun-men Wen-yen, when asked "What is the Buddha?" replied, "An arse scraper."[6] This emphasis on excrement, which might appear gratuitous, is, in fact, a key to understanding Zen and, more widely, a key to understanding what an affirmation of the reality of oneself and one's world might be like. For we devote great efforts to disguising or forgetting the fact that we piss and shit. To remember that is to remember that we are animals, not minds, and that the world stinks in a way that texts do not, except if the latter are employed as arse-scrapers. Zen emerged in China from a synthesis of Buddhism and Taoism, and there is a similar affirmation of the real, couched in similar terms, in the works of the great early Taoists. The *Chuang Tzu*, for instance, contains this key passage:

> Master Tung-kuo asked Chuang Tzu, "This thing called the Way [Tao]—where does it exist?"
>
> Chuang Tzu said, "There's no place it doesn't exist."
>
> "Come," said Master Tung-kuo, "you must be more specific!"
>
> "It is in the ant."
>
> "As low a thing as that?"
>
> "It is in the panic grass."
>
> "But that's lower still!"
>
> "It is in the tiles and shards."
>
> "How can it be so low?"
>
> "It is in the piss and shit!"
>
> Master Tung-kuo made no reply.[7]

The point is that the Tao, which is "highest," is in the lowest. Now it will be immediately evident that if one took this seriously, there would *be* no high or low any more, that such a passage has the potential to shatter one's values. The *Tao Te Ching* says, "When the Tao is lost, there is goodness."[8] Where there is goodness, there the world has been left behind, judged, found wanting. Where there is goodness, there are programs for making things good; goodness improves the world. But, as Lao Tzu also says, "The world is sacred; it can't be improved" (chap. 29). That goes for the piss and shit as well as virtue and beauty.

Indeed, Zen might be called the art of immanence, the art of being within and staying within the world. The Vietnamese Zen master Thich Nhat Hanh puts it like this:

While washing the dishes, you might be thinking about the tea afterwards, and so try to get them out of the way as quickly as possible in order to sit and drink tea. But that means that you are incapable of living during the time you are washing the dishes. When you are washing the dishes, washing the dishes must be the most important thing in your life. Just as when you're drinking tea, drinking tea must be the most important thing in your life. When you're using the toilet, let that be the most important thing in your life. And so on. Chopping wood is meditation. Carrying water is meditation.[9]

What Thich Nhat Hanh calls "mindfulness" is the attempt to experience what is really happening at each moment; it is a call back into ourselves and into what is really here now. It is a defense of the real against the assaults of the past and the future, the reverie and the fantasy, the moral judgment and the scientific description, the evasion and the denial. "Meditation" in this sense results from a resolution to experience the real precisely as it is, to open oneself to it and to proceed into it.

That is why the typical Zen device is meditation on a *koan* (a paradox or non sequitur). To "learn" Zen is to learn how to forget concepts and live in the contingent and particular—in short, to live in the world. Every concept threatens the human connection to the real; every generalization threatens our experience of particularity. We retreat from the realm of things into the realm of concepts because no one has ever been bitten by a concept, because living in the mind is safer than living in the world, or so it appears to be. Indeed, human beings invented language, conception, generalization, mathematics, not as an adaptation to the world; the world always appears in particulars. Rather, *Homo sapiens* must develop consciousness because it is the most *sensitive* animal, the most *vulnerable* animal. Thinking is not a real protection from the world in this vulnerability but an attempt to ward it off. Indeed, consciousness might be the sickness of which we all perish, by which, finally, we detach ourselves from reality in the only way we can ever become detached from reality: by dying. All consciousness is a premonition of extinction; every concept smells of death.

One often hears that it is our capacity for generalization, induction, abduction, and so forth that accounts for our "success" as a species. That is, we can "learn the lesson" of experience by generalizing it to similar situations. Watching Og get eaten teaches us all not to tease bears. But each generalization is also an abandonment of the particular, and an insufficient awareness of the particular is fatal as well. Retreating into laws, concepts, principles, and so forth is all very well; meanwhile, the particular and contingent explodes moment by moment into one's life. "Abstraction" is not only a particular mental capacity; it is a particular state of mind: the one that pitched Thales into the well. At the least, there is something rather sad about missing one's life as one rummages around in general principles.

Zen seeks to bring us back to ourselves and our world out of our abstraction. In the Zen classic *The Platform Sutra of the Sixth Patriarch*, it is said that "From the outset Dharma [the real law] has been in the world. . . . Hence, do not seek the transcendental world outside, by discarding the present world itself."[10]

If Zen teaches us to get beyond, or before, concepts, it is not surprising that one device it uses is shock. D. T. Suzuki relates the following typical tale. When Rinzai was a student, he asked his master Obaku, "What is the fundamental principle of Buddhism?" Obaku replied by striking Rinzai three times.[11] That constitutes a reply to Rinzai's question on several levels. First, it is an enactment of the first of Buddha's Fourfold Noble Truths, that life is suffering. If you would like to *know* that life is suffering, one approach would be to read the sutras, or perhaps you could turn to historical accounts of war, famine, and so forth. You might come, by such a technique, to be able to defend the claim that life is suffering. But in order to *know* it, to know exactly what that really means, it is better to be struck, actually to be in pain. Second, striking Rinzai was a way of telling him that his problem was concepts, that he suffered from an excess of thinking. If you want to achieve enlightenment, you cannot do it by "figuring it out." ("The Tao that can be spoken is not the real Tao.") You cannot think your way to enlightenment, because even if you actually found out what enlightenment was, you would have prohibited yourself from enacting it precisely by conceptualizing it. Enlightenment consists of letting go of concepts into an ecstatic identification with what is; you cannot be further from enlightenment than when you have figured out enlightenment. And lastly, striking someone is a way of "waking them up." Shock has the effect of recalling us to immediacy and rendering us alert to what comes next. To strike someone is to "bring them back to themselves," as we sometimes slap people who are in a tizzy in order to call them back to presence.

That story is typical: Zen masters induce shocks with sticks, hands, projectiles, or anything that's convenient. Here's a particularly extreme case, also related by Suzuki:

> Ummon (Yun-men) was another great master of Zen at the end of the T'ang dynasty. He had to lose one of his legs to get an insight into the life-principle from which the whole universe takes rise, including his own humble existence. He had to visit his teacher Bokuju (Mu-chou) three times before he was admitted to see him. The master asked, "Who are you?" "I am Bun-yen (Wen-yen)," answered the monk. . . . When the truth-seeking monk was allowed to go inside the gate, the master took hold of him by the chest and demanded: "Speak! Speak!" Ummon hesitated, whereupon the master pushed him out of the gate, saying "Oh you good-for-nothing fellow!" While the gate was hastily

shut, one of Ummon's legs was caught and broken. The intense pain resulting from this apparently awakened the poor fellow to the greatest fact of life. (*The Sense of Zen*, 12)

Ummon hesitated because, fearful of saying the wrong thing, he was thinking about what to say. Bokuju makes him pay for his hesitation, because he could not simply speak, or act, spontaneously, as one thing among other things in a world of things. Rather, Ummon separated himself from things in thought, and so debilitated himself in the world.

Now it must be said that what the Zen monk seeks, what Ummon sought when he wanted to see Bokuju, is something we all already possess. We are all, already, utterly absorbed in and by the real. It is the impression, the feeling of distance from the real, that must be dealt with and which the Zen master deals with in the most compelling way by inducing shock. The shock of having his leg broken calls Ummon into reality. But every shock is such a call: everything that is experienced as a shock is, in that sense, the occasion of an enlightenment. Thus, we find joy and reality at the site of great pain:

When [Jo] was passing over a bridge, he happened to meet a cart of three Buddhist scholars one of whom asked Jo: "The river of Zen is deep, and its bottom must be sounded. What does this mean?" Jo, disciple of Rinzai, at once seized the questioner and was at the point of throwing him over the bridge, when his two friends interceded and asked Jo's merciful treatment of the offender. Jo released the scholar, saying, "if not for the intercession of his friends I would at once let him sound the bottom of the river himself."[12]

What this passage says is that the deepest wisdom is found not inside one's own skull but out there, in the real.

The depth of Zen is not a conceptual profundity but a depth in the world. The deepest wisdom is to turn out of one's impoverished imagination and one's impoverished conceptualization and into reality. That is the source of all our real fears but also the source of all our real pleasures. Wisdom is found, if anywhere, right where we already are: crossing a bridge, washing the dishes.

When a disciple asked the Zen master Chao-chou, "What is the one ultimate word of truth?", Chao-chou replied, "Yes."[13] The realism I have been setting out here is a way of saying yes to the world. "Realism" in this sense does not refer to a doctrine or a system. Rather, it is a "position" in the sense of a posture, a physical posture of openness to the world in experience. It is a resolution to experience whatever comes, an acknowledgment of vulnerability. The odd thing about shock is that it shows that we are all already realists. We are always, while we live, open to what is. As Santayana puts it:

> The first thing experience reports is the existence of something, merely as existence, the weight, strain, danger, and lapse of being. If any one should tell me that this is an abstraction, I should reply that it would seem and abstraction to a parrot, who used human words without having human experience, but it is no abstraction to a man, whose language utters imperfectly, and by a superadded articulation, the life within him. (*Scepticism and Animal Faith*, 190)

All fantasies, finally, are over; in the long run, delusions break down before the onslaught of the real. That life calls forth language rather than the other way around is an insight to which we shall return in a discussion of the thought of the Lakota.

And if there is pain in vulnerability, there is also joy. To acknowledge one's powerlessness before the real is to bring oneself into authenticity, to bring oneself into a real relation with the real. For notice: Fantasies may be comparatively harmless, but delusions exact a hideous price. There is, first, the incredible cognitive cost of maintaining them in the face of one's experience. Second, there are, in them, the very limitations one finds in oneself: Delusions and fantasies are impoverished, because the human imagination is small, and is parasitic on the real. To acknowledge reality and one's vulnerability to it, then, brings with it the sort of relief that is characteristic of all expressions of personal authenticity; the cost of lies is high.

And second, the world not only crushes, it caresses, and its beauty, though terrible, is real and absolutely compelling. I cannot fantasize, say, a huge bank of clouds: I cannot produce a mental image, or, for that matter, a text, of the required elaborateness. But I can *see* a bank of clouds, a forest, Times Square, with a robustness and an elaboration that shame any image or text I could ever make. The world destroys us, but compensates us in our destruction by real, rather than imaginary, experiences.

III.

The clearest statement of the sort of realism I am putting forward here is found in Nietzsche's doctrine of the eternal recurrence, a doctrine that Nietzsche himself regarded, with good reason, as his greatest and also his most abysmal thought. Here is the statement of it that appears in *The Gay Science*:

> *The greatest weight*—What if some day or night a demon were to steal after you into your loneliest loneliness and say to you: this life as you now live and have lived, you will have to live once more and innumerable times more; and there will be nothing new in it, but every pain and every joy and every thought and sigh and everything unutterably small or great in your life will have to return to you, all in the same succes-

sion and sequence—even this spider and this moon-light between the trees, and even this moment and I myself. The eternal hourglass of existence is turned upside down again and again, and you with it, speck of dust!

Would you not throw yourself down and gnash your teeth and curse the demon who spoke thus? Or have you once experienced a tremendous moment when you would have answered him: "You are a god and never have I heard anything more divine." If this thought gained possession of you, it would change you as you are or perhaps crush you. . . . [H]ow well disposed would you have to become to yourself and to life *to crave nothing more fervently* than this ultimate confirmation and seal?[14]

If you came to desire nothing more fervently than the eternal return of the same life, you would have learned to affirm your life and the world with a total affirmation. But Nietzsche, quite rightly, describes this thought as "crush-ing." It is even hard to become aware of just how far we are, at any given moment, from this particular sort of joy, from this perfect declaration of love for what is. What if I were now given a second chance at life, and given also the abil-ity to make a different decision at each fork in the road? I would not—indeed, could not—make the same choices again.

Here's an example. My brother Bob was murdered after he drove away from me in a truck with his mur-derer. Knowing what was going to happen, could I have let him drive away? Could I reach the state in which I would make such a choice—choose, in other words, to live my life again as I have lived it? Would I want to become a person who is capable of making such a choice? How well-disposed would I have to be to life to allow myself to experience my brother's death over and over and over in eternity?

This is a way of asking, with the greatest possible intensity, whether I can bring myself to affirm the world, whether I can drag myself back, kicking and screaming, from the fantasy, the narrative, into things as they are precisely as they are. Notice that Nietzsche does not give us an ontology or a narrative here; notice that he does not tell us *what* will be repeated, except that it will be whatever is actual. Nietzsche could have paused here and constructed a little metaphysics, could have *instructed* us in the nature of reality. Instead, he makes a demon *confront* us with what *we know* to be real. This conceptual exercise has a way of making all the dross and gloss fall away, so that if you take it seriously and live with it over a period of time, it *teaches* you what is real: namely, what would be repeated, if your life as a whole were to be repeated.

The movement toward an affirmation of the recurrence, then, is simply a movement of opening to the real. This movement, in a way that is rare or perhaps unique among philosophical thought-experiments, refuses any replacement of the real with a conceptualization. On the contrary, it is designed to compromise all concepts and, finally, to compromise every movement outside or beyond the actual. It is as if at every moment at which one seeks to transcend or even forget the world, the eternal return pulls one back into the world, and embeds one there utterly. The eternal return replaces the afterlife with this life: It condemns you to live *this very life* again and again eternally, and thus shows you how hostile you are to the life you are living and to the world in which you are living it. What it asks, finally, is whether you could reach a moment at which you look at this condemnation as a reward, a moment at which the prospect of living the same thing again and again in eternity can be met with total joy, total commitment, a moment at which love of the world ceases to be a vague fuzzy feeling and attains a perfect specificity.

The eternal return perfectly encapsulates Nietzsche's philosophy, as Nietzsche insisted. Everything that is lovely and joyful in Nietzsche flows from the possibility of that moment in which the return can be affirmed. Notice, to begin with, that the eternal return immediately carries us into a realm in which good and evil no longer make any sense. To say of everything that has been that we welcome it again and again in eternity is absolutely to eschew moral judgments. Nietzsche does not ask us to affirm our lives *for the sake of some epiphanic moment,* or *as a means of transcending those very lives*; rather, he asks us to affirm our lives *in toto* and to love them enough to welcome their return. Thus, our moral judgments will be, in one sense, destroyed utterly. If I could *welcome* my brother's murder, I certainly would have arrived at a place beyond good and evil.

Notice, however, that I did not welcome my brother's murder when it actually took place. I was so full of rage at the time, I think I proposed to myself that if I had the strength I would destroy the world. For that is what happens in extreme cases of moral indignation or moral rage: The object of rage always gets generalized into the real as a whole, so that an anathema is pronounced over the world in its entirety and not simply over the actual occasion. This in itself is a symptom of our "adaptive" capacity for generalization, and it brings us very quickly from a few untoward incidents to a total hatred of the world. That, of course, is the story of various religious interpretations of reality, various philosophies, and so forth. But now notice that this rage at the whole world, for being a world in which my brother was murdered, was, in fact, part of my life. So, were I now to affirm the eternal return, I would have to affirm *those feelings* as well, that total moral outrage, that total negation of all that is in one ecstatic consignment of everything to an imaginary perdition.

So that becomes as deep a challenge as anything in the life of someone, such as Nietzsche, who wants more than anything else to learn to affirm the world precisely as it is: To affirm that, he must also, simultaneously, affirm his own denial of the world. Not only that, but he must affirm the hatred of the world that he finds in Christianity, Buddhism, and so forth: He must affirm precisely that which he most hates. The eternal return confronts us each with precisely that challenge: the challenge to affirm what we hate, which is, then, the challenge to affirm that we cannot affirm, to affirm ourselves as haters. Thus, the eternal return confronts not only all moral judgments; it confronts *itself* as an affirmation of what is; it takes us straight into the heart of the maelstrom in human beings in which values are made and in which values are violated. We must learn, that is, to affirm our hatreds and to affirm, at the same time, the existence of what we hate; it is necessary that we hate, and our hatred will be repeated times without number. But it is also necessary for that which we hate to exist and to be hateful to us.

Thus, we are called into a sort of hatred that refuses to imaginatively destroy the hated object. This is a hatred beyond good and evil, a hatred that refuses to say of the object of hatred, "That ought not to be." For thus is hatred made moral; morality is hatred that says of what it hates, "That ought not to be," and says of what it values, "That ought to be," even when it is not. Now, as I affirm my life in eternity, I will affirm the imaginative annihilations I have performed in the past, *but I will make myself incapable of such annihilations in the future.* If I could reach the moment where I could say "Yes," then I would be saying "Yes" to every moral judgment I or anyone else had ever made. But I would have rendered myself beyond ethics by affirming utterly the existence of what I hate, and the nonexistence of much that I (would) value.

This is what Nietzsche means when he begs us to "remain faithful to the earth."[15] Nietzsche was not a hater of faith; he was a hater of illusion. Truth is found in keeping faith with the world, in not allowing oneself to commit oneself to other worlds. This, of course, entails rejection of the "human spirit," of God as spiritual, of the afterlife for spirit, and so forth. But it entails, as well, a shattering of morals, a suspicion of science, a total affirmation of the world and of life as something in which I am inextricably implicated. The eternal return shows us what it would be like to live in accordance with Zarathustra's deepest teaching:

> Let your gift-giving love and your knowledge serve the meaning of the earth. Thus I beg and beseech you. Do not let them fly away from earthly things and beat their wings against eternal walls. Alas, there has been so much virtue that has flown away. Lead back to the earth the virtue that flew away, as I do—back to the body, back to life, that it may give earth a meaning, a human meaning. (76)

For Nietzsche, virtue is an expression of love and of hatred, of resentment and the strength to make resentment over into value. But a virtue that is "moralized" is a virtue that has turned against the earth and against the body (which is the human being as earth), a virtue that wants, above all, to be elsewhere and that learns to hate all the real as that which imposes this constraint.

Nietzsche teaches us to allow our hatred and our love to return us continually to the world and to situate us in the world ever more inextricably. For, as I will discuss later, hatred and love are both, primordially, acknowledgments of the real in the sense that what is hated or what is loved, like what shocks us, must be experienced as real. But great hatred moves us to avoidance; in hatred, we slowly or quickly become intolerable to ourselves as hateful. And love faces the opposite problem; the defects of the beloved are intolerable to a certain sort of love; love "idealizes" and hence floats free of reality. But at their centers, hatred and love are merely illustrations of our responsiveness to reality: They show us as people who are profoundly moved by what is, who live deeply in this world. Thus, hatred and love, vice and virtue, call us back continually into the world. Nietzsche asks us to use our hatred and our love this way: to allow them to call us back to the earth and back into our bodies.

Nietzsche, hence, does not teach that the earth is good, or beautiful, he simply teaches that it is. And if he teaches us that we will come to be situated on this earth in precisely the way we are now, again and again in eternity, he does so in order to show us that we, too, are. That is Nietzsche's "discovery," which, of course, is something we already know. But the hardest thing for a human being to be is something that *allows* himself *to* be. Every program of self-transformation involves oneself saying to oneself: I ought not to be what I am; I, who am this, ought not to be. Every program of world transformation involves saying to the world: You ought not to be what you are; you, who are this, ought not to be. Nietzsche, like the Zen master who hits you with a stick, calls you to that shattering moment when you can say: I am, and the world is. This is to allow oneself to experience the greatest pain and, thereby, to arrive at the greatest joy. But one does not experience the pain for the sake of joy, else the joy never arrives. One learns to live in pain, and then joy arrives in the body, from the earth.

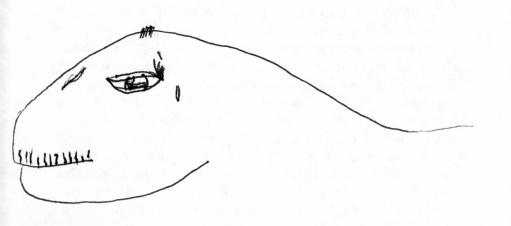

2

Truth, Home, Situation

Now Santayana's line of thought—the view that realism is established by the experience of shock—may look, to put it mildly, unphilosophical. Sitting in your study (insulated precisely from shock), running through arguments, there is nothing you can *do* with shock. Shrieking despair cannot be embodied in a premise: It can't be converted into logical notation and remain shrieking despair. So shrieking despair is not going to help you deduce the existence of objects external to the mind, for example. It is all very well to tell me to drop a bowling ball on my foot, but *in my capacity as a philosopher* this does not seem as though it will help me answer the sceptic.

Of course, one of Santayana's points is that I cannot "in my capacity as a philosopher" cease to be a man, though perhaps seeking to cease to be a man is precisely why I developed a philosophical capacity in the first place. If I am a philosopher, then when I drop a bowling ball on my foot, I am dropping it on the foot of a philosopher, and when I am in shrieking despair, a philosopher shrieks and despairs. Here, however, I would like to pursue another reply to the charge that treating shock as an answer to scepticism is unphilosophical. The use of shock as a demonstration of realism emerges from a philosophy of what human beings are in relation to the world.

If I were a spectator of the world, watching Cartesian ideas unfold as on a movie screen and inferring from them that there are certain things happening out there, then I might need or want an *argument* for the existence of those things. But, as Santayana beautifully says, "I am not a spectator watching this cataract, but a part of the water precipitated over the edge" (*Scepticism and Animal Faith*, 140). That is, I am *fused* with the world I am experiencing; the locus of "my" experience is not within me at all; experience is something that occurs *between myself* and my environment; it is a feature of the situation in which I am embedded. (It would perhaps be truer to speak of me as an embeddedness in a situation rather than as something embedded.) As Emerson puts it, in a passage lifted from the *Bhagavad Gītā*: "The act of seeing and the thing seen, the seer and the spectacle, the subject and the object, are one" ("The Over-Soul," 386).

And he writes:

A man is a bundle of relations, a knot of roots, whose flowers and fruitage is the world. . . . A mind might ponder its thought for ages, and not gain so much self-knowledge as the passion of love shall teach it in a day. Who knows himself before he has thrilled with indignation at an outrage, or has heard an eloquent tongue or has shared the thrill of thousands in a national exultation or alarm? No man can antedate his experience, or guess what faculty or feeling a new object shall unlock, any more than he can draw today the face of a person whom he shall see tomorrow for the first time. (254, 255)

This is radical but right. Persons are not things that watch their experiences flicker by; they are things that experience makes. Persons are constituted by their relations to the real. A Cartesian mind pondering itself, in other words, could not by such means come to know itself, because the mind is not a discrete entity that could be yanked out of particular situations. The mind, rather, is a "bundle of relations." It *is* in part what it experiences: physical objects and states of affairs in the world. No man can antedate his experience, because every man is constituted by his experience, and every experience is a penetration of organism by world. Living in the world is like being impaled on a huge spike.

This is not to claim that there is no distinction between a person and the spike on which that person is impaled; it is not to claim that everyone is everything. I am a *particular* embeddedness; that is, I am impaled on a particular portion of the world. Persons are not distinct from the places they occupy, but each person occupies a particular place. As I move through a place, that place literally moves through me. I am partially composed of the air and water I ingest, and the places I occupy are partly composed of the air and water I eliminate. In a thousand ways, my connectedness to places has articulated my life. When the sun rises, I do likewise; when it sets, I fall over. The history of culture could be written as the history of the adaptation of people to places and the adaptation of places by people, or, as Wendell Berry puts it, "an indecipherable pattern of entrances, minds into minds, minds into place, places into minds."[1]

In particular, people seem to carry with them a connection with or a yearning for a home place. The home place is the place for each person where the unity of person and place is experienced with the most intensity, symbolically and actually. The home place is the place one holds "in one's heart," a place "under the skin." The home place *is* the person whose home it is, a place that constitutes and composes a person. It is a place that has shaped a personality; a person is what the home place has made. The home is a place that is wholly familiar; it has been absorbed by the senses, endlessly traversed, inhaled, ingested.

The home place may be experienced as an oppression; it may be loathed. But every loathing of the home place is, to some degree, a loathing of the self for having emerged from that place and for being what that place has made.

Like our childhood, and in our childhood, it created us. Many people have a sense of rootedness in a particular place, a sense that, in this particular geography, they and it are no longer pitted against one another but embedded in an elaborate system of correspondences and interdependencies.

Our experience of home is a way of showing our relation to the world. Though people may come to feel alienated from the places they occupy (this alienation to a large extent constitutes Western cultural history), though they may try to pit themselves against their situation and, finally, against their situatedness in general (the "soul" is not physical, hence not situated), they are all the time articulated within situation. What I am is not an independently existing item that I could apply to this or that situation in which I find myself; there is no core "me" that reacts in different ways in different situations; "I" at any given point am what the situation is making of what situations have made. Again, that is not to deny my own existence; indeed, existence is always in this sense relational, is always *particular* existence, that is, situated existence. Ontology is *in that sense* conventional, though not usually optional: I could divide up objects in different ways for different purposes. But the philosophical tradition is so intent on escaping the world, the situation, that it tries to stipulate absolute ontological distinctions between persons and other things. The notion of "the social" as it emerges in textualism yanks the human out of its worldly context as emphatically as if it were transporting us to the afterlife. This may look like a way to glorify humanity; again, being of the world, being embedded in a particular situation, is experienced as corruption. But this is a hatred for our home place and hence for ourselves.

Indeed, all corruption, all sin, is, finally, finding oneself in an embarrassing situation: *in flagrante*, getting caught (by God, say) with your hand in the cookie jar. But being a soul is a protection from sin: As the body fornicates (and

the body can only fornicate right *here*, right *now*, in a particular situation), the soul escapes situation. It is, of
course, no accident that this picture, which can be sustained only in a constant assault on one's own experience,
emerges from and intensifies the deepest sort of self-
loathing. The truth is: I am a thing that fornication has
made.

We create "artificial" environments for ourselves not
because they are more convenient but because they allow
self-forgetting. We are seeking our souls, or, rather, seeking
to make ourselves over into souls. More and more of our
experience, for example, is electronic: televised, computer-
ized, and so forth. We seek such experiences, as well as the
more mundane technological articulations of experience
such as the shopping mall, in an attempt to desituate, dis-
embody ourselves, just as we hide excretion in a chamber. Now all of this is, as Emerson points out, futile. We can
deodorize, pomade, dress however we please; it is an animal that we are deodorizing, pomading, dressing up:

> Things are so strictly related, that according to the
> skill of the eye, from any one object the parts and
> properties of any other may be predicted. . . . We talk
> of deviations from natural life, as if artificial life were
> not also natural. The smoothest curled courtier in the
> boudoirs of the palace has an animal nature, rude
> and aboriginal as a white bear, omnipotent to its own
> ends, and is directly related, there amid essences and
> billetsdoux, to Himmaleh mountain chains, and the
> axis of the globe. ("Nature," 548)

Clothing and the creation of artificial environments
are often represented as necessities of survival; obviously,
we take them well beyond the demands of survival and
into an attempt to transform ourselves. This attempt is
always an imaginary desituation, whether the medium is
television, video games, the mansion, the BMW, or high

fashion. The climate-controlled automobile provides me with no particular productive advantages; it simply allows me to forget where I am. What we find "comfortable" is what we find lets us pretend to float free from our bodies, whatever deimplicates us in the world. We do not only produce systems of doctrine, philosophies, religions, in order to make ourselves into something other than bits of the world; the huge belligerent machinery of technology is trained on the same target.

Shock is relevant here as breaking in to our climate controls. And people, often intentionally, leave these "creature comforts" behind in an attempt to find "reality" or "nature." In circumstances in which we have tried so prodigiously to desituate ourselves, we yearn for utter situatedness, and we seek it in forests, atop mountains, on the water, and so forth. There is a pleasure in having one's comforts *interrupted*, in spending all day simply trying to meet one's animal needs. For such reasons, too, I take an especial pleasure in thunderstorms: They demonstrate my continued vulnerability to the real. This pleasure is both made available as a pleasure and attenuated by the fact that I can seek shelter; I am dancing in the storm but dancing in my back yard.

Every feeling of identity with what is is at once deeply satisfying or "spiritual" and deeply threatening; every experience of oneness with what is is also a threat to one's distinctness; that is, it threatens one with annihilation. Death is precisely a loss of individuality, a merging back into things as a whole. In this sense, every making of distinctions, and particularly every distinction made between oneself and the world, oneself and others, is an expression of life, of the resistance of what is alive to annihilation. And to different degrees, everything that we might recognize as a discrete object resists being pulverized; that fact *is* its distinctness. Thus, the attempt to desituate oneself—and Western culture displays great devotion to this end—is an expression of life and, in that sense, of value. The problem is simply this: Life itself always takes place in a situation; there is no organism without an environment. So when we get to the point of fleeing our situation entirely as an expression of the life within us, life has turned against itself; life at that point can't live with itself; perhaps it's gotten too intensely alive to live. Desituation ends in suicide, and suicide is always the most intense expression of life: One commits suicide because there is no escape from one's life, because one feels one's life and hence one's situation with so much acuteness, because one is so sensitive to life. Thus, the attempt to desituate us technologically may end in our deaths. This is no mere after-affect. We are technologically oriented because we hate our situation; we poison it, literally; we try to destroy the situation in which we find ourselves in an effort to become creatures that can transcend particularity.

Our oneness with things expresses itself, for Emerson, in the fact that we are the world in germ, that the inner is a synecdoche of the outer, the outer an elaboration of the inner:

> The world globes itself in a drop of dew. . . . So do we put our life into every act. The true doctrine of omnipresence is, that God reappears with all his parts in every moss and cobweb. The value of the universe contrives to throw itself into every point. ("Compensation," 289)

It is worth discussing for a moment the fact that Emerson talks here of God. And, in fact, throughout his career, Emerson talked of God, and his most characteristic assertion is that the order of nature is a reflection or embodiment of the order of spirit, that the visible embodies the invisible. One rather odd thing about his treatment of this topic is that Emerson, in the course of tens of hundreds of pages, has relatively little to say about God and an inexhaustible appreciation for particular physical facts. He has, I think, no interest in God at all *except* as the spiritual source of the physical world. And in passages such as that just quoted, God appears immanent in the world—the passage is pantheistic.

In an atmosphere where to call something spiritual or invisible is to praise it, while to call it particular and physical is to denigrate it, the claim that the world itself is spiritual is a way of exalting the real. This is typical, for example, of pagan religions, which "spiritualize" concrete objects and forces of nature into Gods, and then worship them as manifest in those very objects or forces. Australian aborigine and Native American religions are good examples here, and I will return at much greater length to the latter. But Emerson is a sort of monotheistic pagan in this regard: The claim that everything is God or expresses God is the pretext for Emerson to go about his actual business—the explication and veneration of the world.

To return to the thread: We not only know the real, we are real, and our animal intelligence in the world is an encapsulation of the world itself. Here is Santayana: "I am myself a substance, moving in the plane of substance, not on the plane of my map; for neither I nor the rest of substance belong to the realm of pictures, nor exist on that scale and in that flat dimension" (*Scepticism and Animal Faith*, 207). And in *The Life of Reason*, he says, "Thought is a form of life and should be conceived on the analogy of nutrition, generation, and art."[2] Like these other functions of the human body, thought arises out of, absorbs, extrudes, reproduces, and handles the real. Thought does not distinguish us from the order of nature any more than does eating or sex; it implicates us in the real ever more utterly.

Notice that, throughout the history of Western philosophy and religion, it is precisely thought which is supposed to desituate us from the order of nature, just as it is the application of thought to nature—technology—that is supposed to liberate us from it. We pride ourselves on being thinking things: No source of human pride is more prevalent than intellect. That thought occurs in nature at all is the philosophical problem of the West; every other problem is a permutation of this problem, or a symptom of it. The interesting thing is not providing a solution to this problem but placing the problematicity of the problem into question. Why, exactly, would it occur to a mammal that one of its functions was incompatible with its being an animal?

Consciousness *nags*; consciousness, once started, is extremely hard to turn off, and, often, is either utterly useless or totally counterproductive. It is a familiar fact that intense self-consciousness is incompatible with decisive action (such facts should be emphasized wherever one hears consciousness spoken of as "adaptive," or perhaps even, bizarrely, the signal of our dominion over the world). Consciousness freezes and debilitates; the man who acts decisively, or who is fit to lead, is never burdened with too much consciousness. I speak from experience when I say that consciousness all too easily becomes a burden to an animal who is obliged to act. Consciousness freezes us by giving us what is apparently a menu of options, and once action is taken, it freezes us again in second thoughts and regrets. At that point, it stands *in need of explanation*.

And the structure of consciousness itself is "distanced," "pictorial," and for that reason always threatens us with certain derangements which are (it is true) not known to other animals. There are people for whom consciousness becomes an absolute barrier, who cannot reach the world consciously. Consciousness, even when it is operating in health, apparently removes us a bit from our situation. And once this removal has begun, it is not easily stopped; in that sense, we are all more or less schizophrenic. Consciousness becomes consciousness of the *possibility* of evasion of the world. And then, by an easy inference, we come to believe that it actually does remove us from the world, that it is not an animal function at all. In the doctrine of the immortal soul and in the doctrine that the body is a text there is always visible the consciousness that has become intolerable to itself and hence intolerant toward the world.

II.

'Truth'—notoriously, I suppose—is an ambiguous term. At times it is used synonymously with 'what is real.' 'The Truth' is just the way things are. Richard Wilbur writes: "We milk the cow of the world and as we do/We whisper in her ear, 'You are not true.'"[3] 'True' in this sense can be used as an adjective that directly modifies nouns that do not refer to propositions, as in the phrase 'true love.' True love is *real* love, sincere love, intense love, and so forth. 'Truth' here is actuality or authenticity. 'Truth' also, and relatedly, has the sense of 'faith,' as in such locutions as "I'll be true to you." Essentially, this means "I will keep faith with you." To be "true" in this sense is to *be* real or authentic or, perhaps, honest. In this sense also we speak of "living in truth" (Havel), or "living truly." 'True' has also the sense of 'precise' or 'exact'; a true line is a straight line. In this sense, truth is to be opposed to all fudging and ambiguity; truth is what is *clear*. Finally, we often use "truth" as a propositional modifier, or (perhaps) operator. Frege, for instance, had an "assertion stroke" in his symbolic logic which meant "It is true that. . . ." In this sense, it is true that the sky is blue on a sunny day, true that butter is greasy, true that truth is stranger than fiction, and so forth. It is this sense of the term that is usually elucidated when philosophers give "theories of truth," such as the correspondence theory, the coherence theory, the pragmatic theory, and the recursive theory. These are theories concerning *what it is* about a proposition or its relations that makes it true.

I have no wish to enter into a detailed debate about which of these views, if any, is the best (or the true) conception of propositional truth. In some sense, views about truth are bottom-line views; no theory of truth could be shown to be true except by begging the question. And, more relevantly, every theory of truth is an expression of our deepest attitudes toward what is. Theories of truth are, at base, religions: They express our deepest commitments, and they are held, if they are held at all, doctrinally. This is not to say that there are *no* tests for adequacy of theories of propositional truth, or that any theory is as good as any other. For one thing, each theory faces the test of practice: It ought to count as true at least most of the claims that we regard as true. Of course, that is also up for grabs if the philosopher in question is willing to bite the bullet, but let me put it this way: If it turns out that, on your theory of truth, it is *not* true that the sky is blue on a sunny day, it's time to get a new theory. And for another thing, notice that there are various ways of evaluating religions that don't have to do, strictly, with establishing or refuting their assertions. A religion that leads you to practice widespread human sacrifice is suspect, for example (occasional human sacrifice is more or less par for the course). And if I am asking myself whether I want to believe, say, Hinduism, I need to ask *what it would do to me*—what needs of mine it might satisfy, what it expresses about me that I am an adherent of this religion.

Theories of truth could be evaluated along the same lines. And now you are not going to be surprised by the approach I will take to diagnosing theories of propositional truth: I want to know whether they are symptoms of world affirmation or world negation, whether they move toward or away from the world. In that sense, I am asking whether they, or their adherents, are courageous or cowardly. Finally, I am asking whether they themselves keep faith with the real, are *true* in that sense. For notice that we *need* not take the notion of *propositional* truth to be fundamental at all. To be true is to be authentic, or to keep faith, or to be clear: We could start from one of those claims (or others) and build an account of propositional truth from that. In fact, I am going to regard the second sense of "truth" I identified above as fundamental. I ask of a theory of propositional truth that it *keep faith with the world*. And if truth is thus truth to the world, it will equally be obvious that I have some sympathy with the correspondence theory: "To say of what is, that it is, or of what is not, that it is not, is the truth" (Aristotle).

Coherence theories—which hold that propositions stand or fall as true or false by their internal relations to other propositions within, say, a language or a conceptual scheme or a theory or the entire body of human knowledge—always threaten us with "truths" that float entirely free of the world. That is the typical attack on coherence views, but it is hardly an academic counterexample; every philosophical or psychological or religious "system," to the degree that it *is* internally coherent, displays the problem. For every philosophical "system"— think of the grand German hallucinations, of Kant, Fichte, Schelling, Hegel, Schopenhauer, and so forth—owes allegiance to itself and not to the world. Each is a systematic evasion of what is; or rather, each seeks to foreclose on what is before it has shown itself. And each "humanizes" the real: Each makes the world over in the human image, or gives us a man-centered world. But the real is, if nothing else, inhuman (even human beings, who are certainly part of the real, are inhuman in this sense). Each philosophical system is an imposition of will on the world on a vast scale, but is, for the very reason of the vastness, purely imaginary, because the actual scope of human will, as I will try to show later, is minuscule. Each philosophical and religious system is a blimp that floats free of reality. To say of such a thing that if it coheres internally, it is true is, shall we say, false to the world; it breaks trust with the world. And to say of such a thing that, if it is sufficiently coherent, it is true, is to reward it for the intensity of its pathology.

Finally, systematic philosophy is an attempt to figure everything out, to bring everything within the scope of human consciousness and, in fact, within the scope of a single human consciousness, namely, that of the guy writing the system. The comprehensiveness of a system and the comprehension that it allows are, finally, attempts to tame the world, to break it. In this sense, every philosophical system worthy of the name is heroic, and hopeless. The making of systems is the technology of the mind; the attempt intellectually to control the world. To locate truth *within* human conceptual structures is the transcendental condition of the possibility of system; system cannot tolerate excess, transgression, otherness; it either ignores them or explains them away or single-mindedly expunges them. That reality continually erupts into the system—or, rather, into the systematizer—is the intolerable truth that coheres with no system. In this sense, truth is always alien, arbitrary, or, again, inhuman. The insistence on system, such as that represented by the coherence theory, and the continual destruction of any given system are always testimony to the strangeness of truth.

That truth is alien, that we won't know it until it gets here, and that we can only hope to hold ourselves open to it is about as well-demonstrated in experience as anything can be. I could not know, for example, the truth about sex in an anticipatory systematization but only by having sex, being a body having sex, being sex. The deepest problem that arises in my experience is that I falsify it *prospectively*, in an anticipation by system, so that I never, say, experience sex, even while I'm fucking. Letting go into sex is delicious but vertiginous; I am spinning out of my control and into the reality of the other. The truth about sex is that it resists comprehension; or, rather, all the truths of sex resist comprehension: That is why it is the seduction and the fusion *par excellence*. It is impossible, for example, to write the truth about sex.

And that will serve to show also what is wrong with the pragmatic theory of truth, the theory that truth is, as James puts it, "what works in the way of belief." This is deeply and perversely wrong; its negation would be nearer the mark: Truth is what fails to work in the way of belief. The mark of truth is its jaggedness, its cumbersomeness, or its eccentricity. Truth crushes, truth kills, but it rarely works. *We* will have it work, we wish it worked, but truth obtrudes. We construct our schemes as prospective systems: The truth tears them down, and us in the process. (As an aside: I think that's a *good* thing. Howard the Duck was "trapped in a world that he never made," as are we all. Well, I don't *want* to live in a world I make, or that we make together; the world *out there* is much more interesting than anything we could have dreamt up.) The truth about truth is, again, this: Sometimes it works, sometimes it doesn't. But every claim that something that *does* work is true needs to be regarded with special suspicion, because we have particular reasons for *wishing* that it were true.

The lesson learned from shock is available everywhere: We are always open to what is. We can construct prospectively: We can create a set of expectations or templates and try to jam actuality into them as we go along. Various theories of perception (such as that developed in E. H. Gombrich's writings) emphasize construction, the expectations represented in concepts, and so forth. But, *of course*, expectations are often frustrated. If I expect to see a frog and instead see a snake, I don't go ahead and think it's a frog. If I expect Fred, and Jed steps into my Fred template, I may momentarily mistake the one for the other, but the world soon corrects me. The most elaborate language, conceptual scheme, or prospective perceptual structure constantly *gives way* before the real, and also emerges out of the real and maintains its connection to it, else it becomes instantly obvious that it is fictional.

I am open to what is: When I see a tree, I do not redesign the branches into a more pleasing arrangement; I am ready to accept whatever particular arrangement the tree provides. The articulation of the world by concepts is a light patina on the monstrous thereness of the real. We notice the concepts, but it is in the real that we have our lives. It is our openness to the world that allows us to survive and that keeps us embedded in the truth.

Finally, though, I would like to cast suspicion on the correspondence theory as well. The truth about sex cannot be embodied in a set of propositions, though perhaps there are true propositions about sex. But locating truth in the realm of propositions, or sentences, is itself problematic. Again, we retreat into pictures or texts to obtain some distance from the real. To make propositions the realm of truth and falsity is thus to remove us as true things from the true and place us in the realm of the proposition, or the "reflection" of the real. Of course, propositions are "abstract" objects; the very same proposition appears here, appears there, is now expressed in French, now in Chinese, and so forth. And such objects are always an embarrassment in that we can't *find* them. But now there are various accounts of the ontology of propositions: I don't know if propositions ought to be in our ontology or not. But that's not the problem. Nor is the problem that propositions, if there are any, cannot be true or false—one stipulates that they *can* be. The problem is making propositional truth fundamental to truth in general.

Rather, I see the truth of propositions as derivative, as derivative from the truth and the faith of the people who make or discover them and from the truth or the faith of the things about which they are made. The *world* is what is true, as love or a line may be true, and to say the truth is to keep faith with the world. To say, "It is true that the sky is blue on a sunny day," is not, perhaps, to say that a certain proposition, 'that the sky is blue on a sunny day,' is true, but to say of something, the blueness of the sky, that it is actual. That is, the sentence may not be about propositions at all but, rather, about the world. That the sen-

tence is true does not necessarily entail that there is something that is true (the proposition) but merely that there is
something that is actual (the blue sky). The truth or falsity
of propositions, on this treatment, would be derivative, or
perhaps a more or less convenient fiction; and calling
something true would always be a way of attributing actuality.

Recall, then, that we, too, are actual; we are true in
that sense: We truly are. Truth is this sort of self-reliance:
Truth is what is given to us in the world, by the world.
Truth is the characteristically human way of being in the
world; as Emerson puts it, "Truth is our element of life"
("Intellect," 424). This is why we think of truth as a *human*
possession of sorts; perhaps that is why we want to
attribute truth to propositions that we invent or discover
rather than to the "things the propositions are about."
When the actuality of things meets human actuality, when
a human being has an authentic encounter with the real,
that person comes into possession of the truth, comes to
truth, or comes to *be* true to things. This requires, or is, at
its center, as Heidegger saw, an openness to things, an
allowance of things to be. There is something at the center
of us that is always receptive and is the "essence" of truth.
Truth is our element of life; it is our aliveness, which is a
responsiveness or a spontaneity within the actual. Truth,
in this sense, is affirmation of what is; truth is what, in us,
affirms what is, and "propositional" truth is the propositional affirmation of what is. No truth, thus, is of human
manufacture; the idealist lives, or, rather, purports to live,
in a "false world," as does the person who locates truth
wholly within social practices.

I think, as I say, that the view of truth that I am developing here has affinities to Heidegger's account. He writes:

All working and achieving, all action and calculation,
keep within an open region within which beings, with
regard to what they are and how they are, can prop-

erly take their stand and become capable of being said. . . . A statement is invested with its correctness by the openness of comportment; for only through the latter can what is opened up really become the standard for the presentative correspondence.[4]

Heidegger is by no means denying that the correctness of propositions consists in their correspondence to reality, but he is asking what it is about us that allows this correspondence to occur, since, after all, propositions are human constructions (or "discoveries," perhaps). And his answer is that it is our openness, or what I have also called our vulnerability, that gives things a place in us, that makes this possible. This sort of openness is unavoidable for living beings, but so is a turning away from this openness. For vulnerability, as I have said, is always problematic for an organism and often intolerable for a consciousness. Thus, it is just what allows us to make correct statements about things that turns us away from truth or conceals things from us. That is the insight that Heidegger develops in his essay on the essence of truth.

Heidegger also says that the essence of truth is freedom. That is because truth occurs in an open region within us; in this sense, to be unfree is to foreclose on the real with concepts or system, while to be free is to allow things to be:

Ordinarily we speak of letting be whenever, for example, we forgo some enterprise that has been planned. . . . To let something be has here the negative sense of letting it alone, of renouncing it, of indifference and even neglect.

However, the phrase required now—to let things be—does not refer to neglect and indifference but rather the opposite. To let be is to engage oneself with beings. . . . To engage oneself with the disclosedness of beings is not to lose oneself in them; rather, such engagement withdraws in the face of beings that they might reveal themselves with respect to what and how they are and in order that presentative correspondence might take its standard from them. (128)

And if truth is freedom, untruth is *submission*. Power—political power, for example—*falsifies* whatever submits to it. To let be is to engage things by renouncing prospective construction: to allow what happens to happen. It is to forsake imaginative compensations for one's vulnerability to the real and hence to allow oneself to experience fully that vulnerability. We are all, while we are alive, real and open to the real. But we can forsake the world imaginatively, or, on the contrary, we can resolve to experience the real and ourselves as real things within the real. This resolution is a letting things be that engages us with the world. And this is the essence of truth, truth as our element of life: truth as that in us which responds to the call of the real, that is capable of celebrating the world. To live in truth, in this sense, is to live in celebration: fully to experience the real by turning oneself constantly toward it.

That is, indeed, freedom, or at any rate a certain sort of freedom. It is not, for example, political freedom or freedom of the will, though it may be freedom from the will or from politics in a certain way. It is freedom as openness, freedom as spaciousness. To experience one's vulnerability to the real is to nurture in oneself a space in which things are allowed to be. And in this place it is possible to play or to dance, to make art, to amuse oneself and others. To nurture this space in oneself is to make oneself vulnerable to pain, but it is also to afford oneself the possibility of joy. There is a difference between the joy of concept, system, imagination, and narrative and a joy taken in the world. Concept, system, imagination, narrative always have the impoverished character of human intelligence but spaciousness in which the real occurs brings to oneself the world's riches. Every "triumph of the imagination" is a narrowing and obscuring of human consciousness, but every allowance of things to be is a liberation of consciousness into the authentic realm of its application. Choreography is always a constraint on human movement; but dance always exceeds choreography, and, at its epiphanies, is experienced fully as a celebration, as something people allow music to do to their bodies.

It is sometimes said of Berkeley's idealism, or Kant's, that whether or not it is true makes no difference to our concrete experiences. Whether that oncoming truck is an external object or something I (or God) has constructed in idea makes no difference to its "appearance" and effects. But the choice between idealism and what I have been calling realism, in fact, makes *all* the difference: the difference between living in an affirmation of the actual in its full-fledged otherness and opacity, living as dance, and living as the center of one's own little choreographed universe. This is the difference between living in and with the truth and living in and with a lie, and is, hence, an example of the deepest human distinction that can be made (which is what the next chapter is about). The failure of idealism, which is also the failure of empiricism, phenomenalism, textualism, and so forth, is, at bottom, a failure to live authentically.

To say the truth, finally, is to *be* true, to speak *out of* the truth, rather than, say, to represent accurately some state of affairs. We are speakers of the truth by virtue, thus, of being true or actual, and in a decision to keep faith with the actual, with our own kind. To be true is to hold open the center of oneself in spontaneity, to allow the tree to display whatever arrangement of branches it displays. To be true, in this sense, also is to withhold judgment by refusing the move into a reconstruction of the actual. Human truth is thus openness, allowance, charity. Such openness requires, more than anything else, a deep courage, for it requires us to be open to our own pain and death within the world.

To say the truth is to participate in what is, to be *true to* the world: It is to keep faith with the world. Thus, to speak the truth is to speak yourself as the world, or as part of the world; it is to be an authentic person. It is, among other things, to be a *particular* person, a particular body, as opposed to a theoretical construct traversing the realm of propositions and evaluating them for accuracy. To be actual, in this sense, is to be *entangled* in the world, *ensnared,* inextricably. To keep faith, for example, with a person requires one to *stay with* that person not only in the sense of being physically present but also in the sense of emotional presence, and in the sense of remaining open to what that person says, how that person moves, what that person *is.* One cannot treat a person with whom one is keeping faith as, say, an example of a neurotic or a hero or a wife. Rather, one must remain there with the particularity of what one is experiencing. And neither can one come to think of oneself as the psychiatrist, the breadwinner, the victim, or whatever; one is required to be precisely— that is, truly—what one is.

Not that there are no isolated truths: not that it is impossible to express isolated facts: "The sky is blue." But to say *that* is to be true, open, for that time and to that extent, to the world. It is true because the world calls upon us to say it. Truth is the world calling us, the world holding us, nurturing us, or crushing us. And it is, likewise, our giving play to the world, us allowing ourselves to be held, nurtured, crushed. Now, in this sense, there is no *escape* from the truth; the world crushes all of us all the time. Every escape from the real is false in that it is not actual; it compensates us in imagination for the world's intolerance. The truth is most of all to be contrasted with the private crochet, the fantasy, the reverie. What is "private" in that sense is not true; what has detached itself imaginatively from the real is, above all, what is false. Truth in this sense is absolutely public; for it is the same world that holds and calls all of us, as we know in our hearts. Emerson says that "no man has a right to perception of any truth, who has not been reacted on by it, so as to be ready to be its martyr" ("Fate," 957). That is true. In a perception of the truth, we are *effaced* before the truth: called into the objective. The truth is, finally, indifferent to our demands—that is its characteristic mark.

And in one of his most profound moments, Emerson adds that "virtue is the adherence in action to the nature of things" ("Spiritual Laws," 320). That is a thoroughgoing reenvisioning of ethics, and it is to reenvisioning ethics that I now turn.

3

Authenticity, Affirmation, Love

If we were seriously, or perhaps light-heartedly, to devote ourselves to the affirmation of what is, we would become sensitive to the elaborateness and the deviousness of the ways in which we negate or evade the actual. Perhaps I would do better to speak for myself: Since I have been seriously and light-heartedly devoting myself to the affirmation of what is, I have become sensitive to the elaborateness and the deviousness of the ways I negate and despise the actual. There are times, indeed, when I no longer know what I can affirm or what it means to affirm or what, if I did affirm, I would leave behind or whether I can affirm what, in affirming, I *have* left behind.

Of one thing I am certain: Affirmation and ethics, as it is usually conceived, cannot coexist. Here is an initial formulation of an affirmation of the real: Whatever exists is good, is beautiful, is right, is perfect. Notice what taking that view seriously would do to ethics or aesthetics or political philosophy. *The Holocaust* is real; thus, it is good. The suffering of the innocent, which the world seems intent on producing in every generation, is right, is good, is beautiful. The starvation of children is good; it could not possibly be better. This, in the words of Leibniz and, more relevantly, Pangloss, is the best of all possible worlds. This is the best, in the abusive locution of Russell, that omnipotence could come up with in eternity. *And yet I am in pain; and yet the innocent suffer.* To call all of this good is to use "good" like an alien; it is to use "good" beyond good and evil.

But to use "good" in this way, one must be prepared to pay a horrible price. To say of this that it is the best of all possible worlds, that this is the best world omnipotence could make in eternity, ought to arouse our disgust. Indeed, in a certain way, no more hateful thought has ever been made public: Any chump could design a better world than this, or, rather, could suggest improvements. To entertain seriously the claim that this is the best of all possible worlds is to be filled with revulsion, not only at suffering and pain and evil but at pleasure and virtue and beauty, which are so paltry and pale and so fearful and world-hating in their actual appearance in this universe. Finally, we will be driven by our thought that this is the best of all possible worlds to find the real world elsewhere, or perhaps hidden within the apparent world.

To say *by our common moral standards*, or for that matter by any standards, that this is the best of all possible worlds will lead us, finally, to the most complete negation of which we are capable. For the world is always that which exceeds or defies any particular standard, so that to say of the world that it meets some particular standard is always to have left the world behind. Indeed, that is exactly why the world is *necessary* to us; otherwise we could simply live in our standards. What is particular about the particular is that it interrupts the application of standards and thus interrupts the sickness that makes us constantly hold reality up to standards, as if God had appointed us to judge the world. The particular calls us out of this delusion, out of ourselves, and into reality.

And yet Leibniz is surely right: The claim that this is the best of all possible worlds follows directly from the existence of an omnipotent, perfectly benevolent God. To believe in such a God, then, is to learn revulsion at the hands of the "best" teacher, to learn it thoroughly and all the time. That this is the world of God's creation—that doctrine ought to end in a hatred of God so intense that eternity could not expunge it. The alternative to that hatred—and hatred is at any rate an authentic response—is living in a hallucination: One has got to "explain away" the most poignant aspects of one's own experience. Shock, pain—whatever it is that one finds intolerable, and hence whatever it is that calls one into the real—that is what has got to turn out to be illusory, or "preparatory," "provisional."

The world can be a horrifying place, but the claim that the horrors of the world are a *test*, a moral *proving ground*, a factory of souls, is truly despicable, or, rather, absolutely intolerable. To regard the world as a moral test will render one's entire life inauthentic. One will always be *on stage*, on the stage of history, playing before the Lord. To regard the world this way is to regard it as a game, though of course a deadly serious game, like a hand of blackjack on which your fortune rides. But to regard the world as a test is to regard oneself with detachment, to live directly away from the particular and toward the criterion. And, of course, that for which one is preparing oneself is the real reality, the reality above and beyond the reality we inhabit. Again, this will turn you away from your own deepest experience as a person. And that, of course, is exactly what beliefs like these are *for*: flight.

In this sense, the soul-making theodicy is typical of all attempts to explain the "meaning" of life. The theodicy is a particularly despicable example, because it explicitly seeks to render us play-actors on a flimsy set, and then asserts—incomprehensibly—that when we arrive at reality, we will be judged on how we have "acted," as if God were a sort of drama critic endowed with the power to punish those whose performance he slams. But all attempts to explain the meaning of life seek to render life false from its roots: radically, irremediably false. Every attempt to give life a meaning is an attempt to permeate life with falsehood from the bottom up. That, of course, is the goal, because one seeks "the meaning of life," only insofar as life as it is actually being lived is intolerable. Always the search for meaning is a cry of pain.

Georges Bataille, whose authorship is precisely a let-ting-go of authorship, of meaning, writes:

> Shouting in the throes of passion, lost in widening
> depths around which lightning plays, can it really mat-
> ter to us *what* is at the bottom of an abyss? Writing, I
> still feel flames, and refuse to go further. What could I
> add? I can't describe the wall of flame that opens in
> the sky—what is suddenly *there*, piercing and gentle
> and simple, unbearable as a child's death. Fear seizes
> me as I write these last words, fear of the empty
> silence I am when face to face with. . . . Determination
> is necessary if a person's to endure a light so blinding.
> Determination not to become weak when a single truth
> is clear—that attempting to enclose *what's there* in
> intellectual categories is the same as being reduced
> to a proud inability to laugh, a result of faith in God.
> To remain a man in the light requires the courage of
> demented incomprehension; it means being set on fire,
> letting go with screams of joy, waiting for death, acting
> in the realization of some presence you don't and can't
> know. It means becoming love and blind light, your-
> self, and attaining the perfect incomprehension of the
> sun.[1]

"The courage of demented incomprehension" is no playful game with the world but a falling into the abyss of the meaninglessness that is there. There is the great joy in "perfect incomprehension" beyond the attempt to make the world over into something meaningful, but to get beyond this is also fully to acknowledge evil, to be pos-sessed of a horror before the real.

For again, to tell us the meaning of life or to make of life a narrative is to tell us that we are not here in the world to be here in the world; it is to hold up the world to a standard, to place existence into the bondage of judgment or submit it to the demands of coherence. We avoid, thereby, a certain dementia. But the arrogance of such a pose is a measure of the extent to which the world is experienced as intolerable, and is so immense that, in the final analysis, it is comic. The world must always disappoint every criterion for judging worlds—that is one way of looking at it. Here is another: The world always defies standards for judging worlds, regards them with total indifference, exceeds them utterly, laughs at them with the demented and intolerable laughter of fate.

One cannot, then, simply hold on to one's notions of goodness and beauty, and then say that whatever exists is good and beautiful, without paying the price of checking out of the world. But there are no other notions of beauty and goodness going. There are no moral systems that are capable of affirming whatever happens to be real: The whole point of a moral system is to sort stuff into the good stuff and the bad stuff: the stuff that *ought to be* and the stuff that *ought not to be*. Simply to say that the stuff that ought to be coincides exactly with the stuff that is would, for the moralist, be violence not primarily to the world but to the moralist. (But the moralist is, after all, part of the world.) And, in this sense, we are all moralists. I remember looking at the body of my brother Bob a few minutes after he had been shot. I felt like tearing the world to shreds, and if I had been telling myself that whatever is actual is good, is beautiful, I would have been engaged in the deepest sort of self-deception or self-destruction. That would have been absolute treason to my experience.

So to affirm the world cannot mean to affirm that the world is morally good. You might have noticed this: The world is absolutely morally blank; the world proceeds in reptilian indifference to our little judgments. I can't *condemn* my brother's murder into nonexistence. But, by the same token, I can't fail to condemn it. To try to expunge it from reality is going to lead me into decades of expensive therapy. But to try to expunge my condemnation of it may hurt me even more severely. I have to be vulnerable to murder; I have to experience the grief, the rage, the screaming moralizer inside that says *this ought not to be.* When I turn aside from that into indifference, much less into ecstatic affirmation, I damage myself as a real person.

I.

So I would like, instead of talking about good and evil, to talk about living in truth and living in lies, to talk about living authentically and living as a fake, a front, a mannequin. Living in truth is living in commitment to the real; it is a resolution to allow the real to be real, to forego all detachment from the real, to live in constant realization of situation. The first thing I am going to try to affirm as I try to affirm things is me. And one thing I must affirm as I try to affirm myself is that I *cannot* affirm my brother's murder. I cannot affirm the Holocaust. I cannot affirm the starvation of children. (Even as I write those last two sentences I am aware—and am horrified by my awareness— that the Holocaust and the starvation of children are abstractions for me now. They are philosophical examples. One thing I will say for my brother's murder is that it steadfastly refuses to become an abstraction for me, even when I write about it. It stays particular and real for me even in the face of philosophy; very few things do.) There are many things about myself—my self-centeredness, for instance, or my alcoholism—that I find extremely difficult to affirm. And yet their jaggedness, their recalcitrance to acceptance, is something I also need. They, too, and perhaps, as I will discuss later, more than anything else, teach me about the real.

For the point is that the evil calls us to reality just as much as the good. What I hate must be experienced by me as real, else I would be incapable of hating it. My hate may make me turn away into fiction in the end, may make me want to deny the reality of the object of my hatred as a way to relieve myself of hatred. But as long as I am resolved to *stay in* my hate, to hold it and experience it until it runs its course, I *ipso facto* hold on to the reality of the object of my hatred. To curse something, to condemn it, is not always "moral"; that is, it does not always consign the hated object into an imaginary perdition, the perdition of what "ought not to be." Hatred is visceral, premoral. What is hated *is*; it obtrudes itself more vividly into our experience than other objects. In this sense, I *need* my hatreds as much as I need anything, and to "moralize" hatred by showing that the object or occasion of hatred ought not to be is always to shunt hatred away.

In this way, the imaginary consignment of things to perdition which is the heart of ethics is itself a testimony to the ineradicable presence of those very things. When I am in the midst of hatred, I am experiencing the hated object as being present, as intensely, pointedly real. When I now seek to jettison that thing into the outer dark where there is wailing and gnashing of teeth, I testify precisely to its ontological exuberance. What is most real to the moralizer is sin. And, indeed, that people are out there committing sodomy, stealing, and so forth, are facts that are wonderfully recalcitrant. Sunday after Sunday, the preachers rail against these facts, pit their hate against this bit of the real. And, of course, people go right on sodomizing one another, a very good idea indeed. Then we simply convey these people, sins and all, to an imaginary purgation. But the fact that we can continue, week after week and day after day and hour after hour, to express our condemnation only shows us the intensity of our hate and hence the intensity with which we experience the real as real. Our hatred and condemnation of the real is constant and extreme, but it is as nothing compared with the real's hatefulness, which continues all day every day everywhere. Pitting our little hatred against the hatefulness of the real is like trying to stop a tank with a pea shooter. But at least it displays our implication in the real in the clearest possible terms.

To hate the real is truer to it than to regard it with indifference, as recommended in Stoicism or in portions of the Buddhist and Hindu traditions. For to regard the real with indifference is (as, indeed, all these traditions emphasize) to learn to regard it as unreal. What is experienced as real is not regarded indifferently, for each experience of the real as real teaches us about our own situation as and in the real. So the Stoic or Vedantic sort of discipline for the treatment of hatred is always articulated as a metaphysics, in which the reality of the real is denied or attenuated. Each experience of the real as real teaches us that we are implicated in the real. Thus, hatred of the body, hatred of sin, and so forth are authentic responses to the reality of the real. Self-loathing and world loathing hold us within the reality of the real.

In other words, moral condemnation is not an expression of hatred (I am agreeing here with the moralists): Moral condemnation is the "treatment" for hatred, a way of ameliorating, repressing, ceasing to experience hatred. Thus, the legal system is, among other things, a machinery for the containment of hatred; its function is to control the hatred of "its" people by moralizing their hatred and expressing it as punishment. That is, the legal system is not devoted to harming the punished but to treating the punisher. Punishment administered by the legal system is inhuman: It is not *me* punishing *you* but the *system* punishing *the offender*, as if concepts could punish concepts. Every schedule of punishments known to man at the present time is an attempt to evade hatred by abstracting from the real. Evasion of hatred is, hence, precisely evasion of the world. To the extent that "culture" requires such machinery, to the extent that a "society" cannot be made without teaching people to evade their own hatreds—to that extent is society inimical to human authenticity.

I might like myself better if I could take my own advice and simply affirm, beatifically, all that is. Then I could be a beautiful soul whom all would admire. The fact that various disciples were prostrating themselves before me would not disturb my celebrated humility and equanimity. Unfortunately, however, I lost my car keys this morning and started tearing up my house. It was the fact that the world was not cooperating with my plans that made me mad; nothing enrages me more than when the world will not conform to my blueprint. Or I should say that one thing makes me madder than that: when *I* fail to conform to my blueprint. I demand an end to my own stupidity.

To treat myself as real, or to be an authentic person, would be to allow my hatred and my stupidity to take me where they may. My hatred and my stupidity, if I could allow myself to experience them fully, would bring me back into the world and to my own situation in the world. Hence, they would bring me back to myself and to my own truth, my own openness to the world, and to myself as part of the world. In the words of Popeye, "I yam what I yam." This is not to say that I am not educable or volatile or malleable or corrigible, but it is to resolve to open myself to myself. To acknowledge one's reality, to experience the fact that one is real, and to *show* one's reality to other persons—these are antiethical or postethical "values." If I am in grief, my grief is real, and I seek to acknowledge what is real, and to pay it honor, for it has the dignity and integrity that is possessed by everything real, even (or particularly) the intolerable.

Mark Twain wrote that "Everybody lies—every day; every hour; awake; asleep; in his dreams; in his mourning; if he keeps his tongue still, his hands, his feet, his eyes, his attitude will convey deception."[2] Now, Twain asserted—whether sarcastically or not is not perfectly clear—that this was a good idea, that civilization would not be possible without each person living and conveying a tissue of lies. That places into question either truth or civilization. Notice, however, that Twain told a deal of truth in his time, and was telling it here. Some lies are propositional, and consist of intentionally uttering a claim one knows to be false. But most lying—and it is this with which Twain concerns himself for the most part—is found in the way we gesticulate or avert our gaze: in short, lying is a way of living rather than simply, say, a morally questionable act. And living a lie is not a matter of asserting what is false, not even to oneself, though it no doubt involves that. Like the truth, the locus of the lie is the region in which the world occurs in people, or is the relation of the world to people, or is a feature of that relation. So, like the truth, the fundamental notion of the lie is a matter not of what people do with propositions but of what they do with the world. To live a lie, in this sense, is to live in closure from the world, to attempt to seal off the consciousness from the real's incursions. It goes without saying that this achievement is always illusory, which is precisely why it's a lie.

One does not, cannot, find the truth within oneself. That is a fundamental mistake of Kierkegaard and other existentialists, who otherwise, I think, are often sympathetic to the approach I am putting forward here. One does not, cannot, consult oneself to find out the truth of oneself; as, again, Emerson said, no man antedates his own experience. We find the truth of ourselves precisely by *being* in the world; our truth is our situation, and an acknowledgment of our truth is, hence, a vulnerability to situation or an allowance of oneself to be situated, an allowance of the situation to be. To speak out of that acknowledgment is to speak the truth. Ultimately, the lie that infects and destroys the self is the closing off of oneself from the real as a treatment for hatred or fear, or perhaps even too-great love, of the real. When one hates, the courage to hate and the courage to express hatred are expressions of truth and, hence, acknowledgments of situation, for, again, hatred always involves an experience of the conspicuous existence of the object of hatred. When one flees hatred, one comes to live a lie, and the only way this can be accomplished is by leaving reality in imagination. Every allowance of oneself to experience the feelings one is having, or simply to experience at all, is always simultaneously an opening of oneself to the world. To be true in this sense is to be and to speak out of the world's truth.

Truth—and I cannot emphasize this enough—is never found by a sheer movement inward, though it may involve reflection. Every movement inward is a (delusory) flight from the truth. To discover one's own authenticity, it is necessary to act and to be acted upon, to allow the world to bring you to truth, or to nurture you in truth, or to crush the falsehood out of you. Finding out "who you are" is a matter not of seeing what you are already but of becoming something by acting in the world and as part of the world. Personal authenticity is hence—and I will explore this in the next chapter—public authenticity. Personal authenticity proceeds from the world and makes its way back into the world. Or better: Personal authenticity is a keeping of faith with the world, a love or hate for a world that is allowed to be what it is.

So I am resolved: not to be a mannequin, a facade, a surface, an act, but to be a man. I am going to attempt to show you what I really am and not what I think you want me to be. I am going to respect my own unity and my own contradictions. I am going to bring myself back into myself, that is, back into what is real.

Now, of course, this is a Pandora's box. What I am might be horrible, sick, cruel. If I simply allow myself to experience my hatred, if I do not treat myself as an abstraction and apply ethical principles to myself, regarding myself as a proving ground or a "moral agent," imaginatively destroying parts of myself or acting as if they did not exist, then God knows where I could end up. I suppose "conscience" would be at an end; there could be no more division of the self against the self as preacher and sinner. And, indeed, the last thing that I want to do is simply assure you that an "ethics" of authenticity is harmless or is itself morally desirable or will lead you to display all the virtues, work for the greatest good of the greatest number, universalize your maxims, and so forth.

But it is worth remarking that we pay a pretty hideous price for our falsity. It is horrible to come to regard the world as something that ought not to be. But it is even more horrible to come to regard oneself as something that ought not to be, so that one is always in the process of morally expurgating oneself, of taking control of oneself. Thus, every moral judgment of oneself is a sort of suicide; ultimately it will render the self inauthentic in the only way anything can, finally, fail to be authentic: by failing to be. That we cannot allow ourselves to experience our own hatreds does not in itself give us something to do with the energy generated by hatred; it merely, in the familiar fashion, displaces it onto other objects, turns it inward on ourselves, and so forth. Hatred of that sort *festers*, as we all know; it grows, finally, until it is a hatred of everything and everyone. That we learn to treat ourselves and one another as abstractions by the activity of moral expression and moral evaluation—this encourages the most horrible acts. We treat ourselves as abstractions when we evaluate ourselves morally; we keep what we like and pretend to jettison what we find wanting. And we treat one another as abstractions when we evaluate one another morally. As we are going to see, as soon as I treat you as an abstraction, I can easily enough justify any treatment of you. As soon as you are "a Jew," "a policeman," "an informer," "a wife," you had better watch out, for now you are no longer a thing existing out there but a marker in my conceptual scheme. Furthermore, I now quickly construct myself as a corresponding abstraction. The very odd thing about all this is that it is impossible for abstractions to be treated wrongly and impossible also for them to treat anything or anyone wrongly. So, in my abstract capacity as a holder of values, I can do anything to you, and you can suffer anything, with impunity; it is no longer *me* raping *you*, for instance, but the husband raping the wife. I have sucked the reality out of you imaginatively and now, if you allow me to (or, for that matter, if you don't), I will suck the reality out of you in fact.

The most intolerable thing for a human being, and I speak here from inside, is to become that sort of abstraction to oneself. And, of course, every system of morality demands precisely that. This has the same results: For notice that as soon as *I* become a Jew, a policeman, a wife, or whatever, I am incapable of any real encounter with anything, being a mere abstraction. So when *in my capacity as a policeman* I beat you to death, I will be *surprised* if I am held accountable. But whatever the outward effects, the impoverishment of inner life is unspeakable. I know how I, in my capacity as an X, *ought to* respond in a given situation, and I respond that way, even at the cost of my self. To take on a role, to live life in one's roles, or to try to live as, or up to, a "role model," is to turn away from one's own life. Each such role infests and falsifies you slowly from the top to the bottom, until you no longer even know what you want, what you fear, what you hate, what you love. Each role tries to turn you from what you are into what you "ought to be" according to the *role's* demands. And to tell you what you ought to be—that entails that you ought not to be, as you are.

Both the sickest and most hopeful feature of this situation is that it is always, by definition I guess, false. You *do* hate what you hate, and "being a teacher," for example, is no real treatment for that hate. "I ought not to do this" is always an invitation to be seduced; "I ought not to feel this" is always an invitation to discharge your feelings on unwary passersby instead of their real objects; "I ought not to think this" is always the first moment of obsession. If you consult your heart, I believe you will find this true: You cannot remake yourself by performing a role. And the measure of your peace, in your role or outside it, will be the extent to which, in your role, you can keep faith with what you are. Emerson says: "No sane man at last distrusts himself. His existence is a perfect answer to all sentimental cavils. If he is, he is wanted, and has the precise properties that are required. . . . We have as good right, and the same sort of right to be here, as Cape Cod or Sandy Hook have to be there" ("Considerations by the Way," 1082).

This is the key thought of Emerson's ethics, an ethics that I believe is one of the deepest and most radical in the history of ideas. For surely, to take the moral status of human beings to be exactly like the moral status of Cape Cod is going to entail some pretty radical shifts in our thinking. Finally, whether we ought to exist and whether, if we ought to exist, we ought to exist as we are (and these finally amount to the same thing) are going to turn out on this view to be *insane* questions. A person who expressed doubt about Cape Cod's right to exist, or who, for that matter, affirmed Cape Cod's right to exist, would be quite mad. *That* it exists ends the discussion.

It is, of course, no mere surface affinity that drew Nietzsche to Emerson; Nietzsche saw in Emerson the possibility of the "revaluation of all values," or a critique of all values as harboring within them the seed of world- and self-hatred. "Sincerity," Emerson writes, "is the property of all things. To make our word or act sublime, we must make it real." Now this sounds salutary, but so far it does not seem to provide an alternative to moral values. For it seems to say that we *ought* to make our world or act real, that we ought to eschew insincerity. However, Emerson continues like this: "Use what language you will, you can never say anything but what you are. What I am, and what I think, is conveyed to you in spite of my efforts to hold it back" ("Worship," 1068). Look. Sandy Hook and Cape Cod are "sincere" in the sense that they *are what they are*. And, of course, that is true of all things, including human beings. To be sincere, in Emerson's sense, turns out to be to be. To be a hypocrite, in this sense, is to try to disguise one's realness; but we are all "ethical," in this sense, *merely by existing*. To assume a "role" is always, hence, precisely hypocrisy and the assertion of what is impossible, because it is always an expurgation of one's reality. In the same essay, Emerson says that the point is to prefer being to seeming.

To be "real" in this sense is to speak the truth and allow the truth to be acknowledged. Emerson writes:

> In all the superior people I have met, I notice direct-ness, truth spoken more truly, as if everything of obstruction, of malformation, had been trained away. What have they to conceal? What have they to exhibit? . . . For, it is not what talents or genius a man has, but how he is to his talents, that consti-tutes friendship and character. That man [who] stands by himself, the universe stands by him also. ("Behav-ior," 1049)

We are all already real. The point is to live in an acknowl-edgment, enactment, and celebration of that fact. This is not something one accomplishes but something reality accomplishes by working into one. And that is something that, as it happens, we all *want*; as Emerson greatly says: "We crave a sense of reality, though it come in strokes of pain" ("New England Reformers," 603). One way we express this craving is in a movement out into the world; it is a craving for engagement with things. But the movement outward, the emptying of the self into the world, is also a movement inward; we crave to engage *ourselves* with things.

In this sense, the task of living in truth, as it faces each person with the truth of herself, is a matter of keeping faith with oneself as a real, situated, particular being. The "ethics" of authenticity emerges, that is, out of a willingness to *hold on* to oneself, to allow oneself to be. I can enter into gigantic programs of self-transformation (and I have), programs to remake my body, my knowledge, my emo-tions, and so forth. Such programs *do* issue in changes of me, though not usually of just the kind I expect. But the fact that I regard myself as something that stands in need of transformation shows how ill-disposed I am toward myself, just as the fact that I regard the world as something that stands in need of transformation shows how ill-disposed I am toward the world. Now, if I were to keep faith with myself, I would have to keep faith with myself precisely as, among other things, a person who continually loses faith with himself. I would have to acknowledge that *I want to be transformed.* But I would need to resolve to allow myself to be, to whatever extent and in whatever ways I can. My power to remake myself is at least as limited as my power to remake my immediate environment; for that reason, many people experience their own continued presence to themselves as intolerable. In fact, I believe all people often experience themselves precisely as something "external" to themselves, something too heavy for them to lift, and so forth. And that is a *necessary* way to experience oneself, for it will teach one an allowance to be, teach one to "let oneself go." Peace flows from letting oneself go, as does humor, for example, which often occurs in an allowance of oneself and the world to be. I need to acknowledge these limits and try to learn to live inside them, since I am already inside them.

II.

Now that I have resolved on a way to treat me, I need to ask how I could treat you and the world. Again, notice that I cannot simply value what is actual as good and beautiful without endangering myself to the utmost or without falsifying my relation to you and to the world from top to bottom. Here I would like to talk about love.

Love is an odd thing. It's not a *virtue* per se; it is something that happens *to* us, not something we make happen or something that can be cultivated. We simply *find ourselves* responding to someone or something with love when we *open ourselves* to them. Of course, at other times when we open ourselves or find ourselves opened to things and persons, we respond with hate. Either lets us feel ourselves in authentic relation to the real. But I am searching here for a mode of *affirmation* that does not involve *falsification*. To say of something that it is good or beautiful is to affirm it, in a certain way. But as we have seen, to say of *the world* that it is good or beautiful could not be to affirm *it*, but is always to leave it behind in the search for something that *is* good or beautiful: heaven, maybe, or a sort of sick parody of the world, which I might then assert the world to be (a testing ground, etc.). And what I want to say is this: I want to learn to love the world.

I think that the Platonic and Neoplatonic conception of love is probably, first, one of the most characteristically philosophical events in Western history and, second, one of the most absurd grotesqueries ever performed. For on this conception, one learns to love the general through loving the particular; one learns to love Beauty by loving the imperfectly beautiful real thing; one learns to love the Ideas by buggery. (Next time you are engaged in buggery, be real enough to notice that it embeds or impales you ever more deeply in or on the particular rather than transports you to the abstract.) Here is a characteristic passage from *The Symposium*, in which Diotima is telling Socrates how to get from appreciation of boys to appreciation of nothing in particular:

> When his prescribed devotion to boyish beauties has carried our candidate so far that the universal beauty dawns upon his inward sight, he is almost within reach of the final revelation. And this is the way, the only way, he must approach, or be led toward, the sanctuary of Love. Starting from individual beauties, the quest for the universal beauty must find him ever mounting the heavenly ladder, stepping from rung to rung—that is, from one to two, and from two to *every* lovely body, from bodily beauty to the beauty of insti-

tutions, from institutions to learning, and from learning in general to the special lore that pertains to nothing but the beautiful itself—until at last he comes to
know what beauty is.

And if, my dear Socrates, Diotima went on, man's
life is ever worth the living, it is when he has attained
this vision of the very soul of beauty.[3]

I don't think words could convey how despicable this passage really is. First of all, notice that love always responds
to beauty on this account. But notice, too, that people
often love other people whether they are beautiful or not.
And notice that the ideal here is to learn to love concepts
and so forth, until one forgets how to love anything in particular, that is, until one loves only and strictly that which
does not exist. It is no coincidence that Diotima betrays the
suspicion that life is not worth living if it is lived in the
particular; the funny thing about this is that life is always
lived only in the particular. It follows from this that, in
Plato's famous phrase, "the philosopher studies to die." If
you become deranged or idiotic enough that you find yourself loving *institutions*, stop there before you learn to love
only strictly fictional entities. (As we shall see, though,
Plato is right about his ontological ladder here: Institutions are more abstract than persons.)

It is worth asking oneself whether, in the process of
"mounting" the ladder, one does not lose one's capacity to
love the particular. For notice that on this view boys are
going to end up looking pretty ugly in comparison with
pure concepts. Boys are messy little creatures; they'll burp
in your face and think it's funny. They're nasty mammals,
but we're learning to love wisps of smoke, or whatever
doesn't confront us with particularity. To mount the ladder
of Love, then, is to learn to hate the world, all of it. Swooning before government agencies would be asinine enough,
but loving abstractions is about as bad as it gets. Or rather,
abstractions are precisely what it is impossible to love; love

is always precisely what holds dear the particularity of the beloved. Love is an opening of the self to the particularity of the beloved, so that love is not an abstraction away from ugliness but an allowance of ugliness to be.

The next time someone to whom you have given professions of love asks you why you love or what you love, try explaining that you love that person as an (admittedly dim and flickering) simulacrum of Beauty or of the Idea of themselves. That is, you love not the person but what the person could be if not circumscribed by particularity and personality—not the person but The Person.

To love Beauty and Persons is, literally, to love nothing; it is to be incapable of love. To love some *one* is to love *some* one, not anyone, or everyone, or no one in particular. Occasionally, you meet people who, searching for someone to love, advance a checklist of attributes: good sense of humor, mid-forties, over seven feet tall, and so on. When a particular person shows up that matches the template: BAM! However, that ain't love, or perhaps it's love of the Form rather than the particular, of nothing rather than something. This sort of "love" is a flight from particularity, or, rather, a flight from one's own particularity. For what we are dealing with here, ultimately, is hatred of the self, or moral expurgation of the self. *My* buggery isn't any particular buggery; what I'm mounting is the ladder to Beauty. I am tired, dead tired, of being particular and being entangled in a web of particular things. What love of institutions, much less of Pure Ideas, expresses is the absolute exhaustion of one's capacity for love. One needs an ever escalating provision of beauty in order to arouse oneself, and finally one cannot make due with the beauty of this world. Jadedness speaks from these claims: a world-weariness that is no longer capable of experiencing the beauty of the particular and compensates itself with fantasy or description.

Particular people are the hardest thing to love; on the other hand, they're the only people that can be loved, because there are only particular people. If I love the general as expressed in you, then I will learn over the long haul to hate you as the corruption of the general, just as if I love the world as God's creation, I will come to hate the world and love God. If I love you while regarding you as what you are not, then do I love you? The challenge of love is to learn what is odd or despicable or just human about the person you love, and to love anyway. I do not love *what is admirable in you*; I love *you*: the whole package. That is why love is something amazing—not because love forgoes judgment or sees only the good but because it sees clearly the reality and still yearns toward it, still affirms it, still holds it in its heart. I do not love you only when you are unconditionally good: I love you whatever the conditions.

We speak of loving people "just as they are." But there is a confusion about this. It might mean to *believe* of someone that that person is perfect—that she (say) is incomparably beautiful, intelligent, and so on. That is, the notion of love is sometimes confused with unconditional approbation, so that to love someone is to believe that they are damn near perfect. However, notice, first of all, that love is not belief but a sort of overflowing of feeling. And notice, too (and this should be familiar), at what cost this conceptual love is purchased. For in order to regard you as perfect, I simply have to exorcise your demons in my imagination; I cannot let you be human. That is, I cannot enter into a relationship with *you* at all, much less love you. To love in this sense is to approve a person in a Panglossian way, just as to judge the world to be good and beautiful is a strange sort of affirmation. What is strange about these affirmations is that they do not affirm the very thing at which their affirmation is directed. They must construct the beloved (the world, the wife) prospectively before they can love. What they ultimately love is not the world or the wife at all but their fantasy, that is, nothing at all.

That is why love, love of real people and the real world, is alternative to ethics. I cannot say that everything that is actual is good. But I can *love* what is for being and in being, even as it causes me immense pain, or even as it drives me to suicide. I can love the world, though it is the world in which my brother was killed. I can love the world, though it is the world that sent six million Jews to the gas chamber. I can love the world, even, and be horrified at myself for loving it (I do and am). The poignancy, the unremitting particularity of the world, is a call to love, and the love it calls out is deep and abiding. We can love only the particular, and we can truly love the particular only if we experience it in its particularity. I love you, though I know that you take the occasional crap. I love you even while I'm yelling at you. I love you only to the extent that I am aware of your "faults" and am still here affirming you. And I have had moments, like that described by Bataille above, in which I love the world to the point of rapture, and these are always when I am looking directly at evil, when I am experiencing reality in its relentless indifference to my values. Nietzsche writes: "Whatever is done from love always occurs beyond good and evil."[4] That is, I love the world only to the extent that, and most at the moments when, I experience those parts of it that are the hardest for me to take, those parts that confront me most viciously with their reality.

If that is an ethics, then I guess it is my ethics, though I am very far from being able to put it into operation. I want to love the world for being real and to love the people in the world for being real and to love the earth for being real. I want to love them *while judging them insufficient*, for I cannot help but judge them insufficient. I want to love them and also rage against them: They have the perfect opacity and the recalcitrance to will that enrages me constantly against them. In *Thus Spoke Zarathustra*, Nietzsche writes that "the lover would create because he despises. What does he know of love who did not have to despise precisely what he loves!"[5] And later he also says: "Deeply I love only life—and verily, most of all when I hate life" (109).

Love here is connected with the call into the reality of the beloved; above all, love sees the beloved clearly. In this sense love is just the opposite of "romance," in which the beloved is turned into a sort of apparition of Beauty. For that reason we *have to* despise what we love, because love calls us into the reality of the beloved, punctures our illusions. All "true love," in this sense, is a keeping faith with the beloved and with the world in the beloved; love does not allow any more illusion, or, rather, leaves illusions beside the point. Love seeks to establish an authentic connection to the reality of the beloved, and hence turns away from imagination toward the actuality of the beloved. We despise what we love as we despise what is most familiar to us, what we know best, and also as we love what is most familiar (as we love and despise our homes, for example).

To love is to allow the beloved to be outside of one's control, or, rather, to acknowledge that the beloved is outside one's control. Heidegger calls freedom—letting things be—the essence of truth, but I would prefer to call this essence "love," though I would, when you get down to it, prefer not to talk about essences at all. But truth happens in us when we allow things to be; there is a space in us of reception, a space in which we give of ourselves to things and in which things take their stand, come to appearance, and so forth. Well, that space is our love; to create that space for someone, or to allow someone into that space, is to allow them to come into love, and it is to come to know the beloved's truth. Science, in this sense, is, at its best, an expression of love for the world: a resolution to open oneself to the world. To love someone is to *allow them in* to where their truth can be experienced in oneself.

To love is to acknowledge the integrity of the beloved: to let the beloved be precisely what it is. To love someone or something is to resolve to let it be; it is to affirm that it is lovable, not if it is perfected or reconstructed or transported to the realm of the Forms but just as it already is. This is not to say, "She whom I love is already perfect," but to say, "I love her though I *must* judge her inadequate or hateful or ridiculous." In this way, as we know, we are always the *victims* of our great loves: We must *let be* that which we can also see must be changed. Every assertion that the beloved is already perfect, or could not possibly be better, is a betrayal of love, just as every assertion that the world could not be better than it is is a betrayal of the world. The point is to *live within* the beloved and for the beloved to live within you, as the point is to live within the world and to let the world be. In this way it is true that, as Nietzsche says, "I love only life," not in that I love life through you but in that insofar as I love you, I respond to your aliveness.

Here, too, is revealed the structure of situation in the world that I described in the last chapter. For in order to love you, I must simultaneously take you up and let you go. I must create a space in myself in which you can stand before me in your reality. I cannot literally *become* you or expunge you, else I have (obviously) ceased to love you. I must allow you to remain *pitted against* me: there, opposite me, being you. That is, I must respect your reality in the sense of acknowledging you to be outside myself. Love is constantly in danger from these two imaginative poles: First, I lose my love if I shunt you away into the realm of the Forms and make of you a perfect woman. To do this is to *fend you off*, to isolate myself in my particularity and imperfection. But second, I lose you (imaginatively) if I *ingest* you, if I try to incorporate you into myself, if "we two become one." This is likewise an expression of intolerance for your realness, though in the first case I abase myself before the perfect and in the second I aggrandize myself by taking you over.

So the structure of lover and beloved, self and other, is precisely the structure of person and world: My situatedness in the world and my situatedness in a human community are of the same sort. And, of course, there is no reason why this should not be the case, since human beings are bits of the world. As I experience my situated-ness in the world not as an immediate merging with all that is or the pulverization of my self, nor yet as a loss or negation of the world by a soul, but as a situatedness by which I am constituted, I experience human relationships not as a merging, nor yet as murder or a negation of per-sons, but as an embeddedness that I learn to experience as love and also hate. Learning to let people be what they are is learning, among other things, the possibility of love.

4

ANARCHY, PARTICULARITY, REALITY

One thing I have been doing in the above discussion is trying to see what happens to us when we eschew abstraction, when we try to treat ourselves and one another not as "the Jew," "the teacher," "the wife," "the policeman" but rather as particular human beings. As I have asserted several times before, concepts are expressions of our vulnerability; abstractions are where we flee when the world of concrete particulars becomes intolerable to us. But we ourselves and the people we have to deal with are also concrete particulars, and few things are more often or more intensely intolerable than people. I am often intolerable to myself, and you are often intolerable to me. So I cease to deal with you and start to deal with a concept under which I can "subsume" you or into which I can annihilate you, so that you live on in the realm of my concepts in a sort of flickering afterlife. The whole science of sociology, with its demographics, polling data, and so forth (and the political life of Western culture has now been almost wholly infected with sociology) is devoted to taking the human individual—bizarre, recalcitrant, stupid, strange—and rendering her comprehensible.

Politics then goes about dealing with people as transformed by sociology into abstractions. One thing, for example, that drove sociologists mad about Ronald Reagan and even George Bush was that people responded to their personalities rather than to their "policies," so that Reagan was well-liked even when people disagreed with him, and they voted for him because they liked him. In fact, looking at someone and seeing that he's a nice guy is, for my money, a more respectable way to choose a "leader" than is the examination of position papers, which always turn out to be empty abstractions couched in the fantasy jargon of sociology. Now I would like to have a go, with the help of Vaclav Havel, at seeing what might happen to politics if we eschewed fantasy and tried to engage each other as flesh-and-blood persons.

I.

It is an odd fact that philosophers such as Nietzsche and Thoreau have expressed doubts not about the legitimacy or the effectiveness of the state but about the state's *existence*. That is, they have had the notion that the state was a fictional entity, a sort of myth or fantasy or lie. Thoreau says:

> To one who habitually endeavors to contemplate the true nature of things, the political state can hardly be said to have any existence whatever. It is unreal, incredible, and insignificant to him, and for him to endeavor to extract the truth from such lean material is like making sugar from linen rags, when sugar-cane may be had.[1]

That the state lies everyone knows only too well; that it *is* a lie is something we may all find out by and by. Nietzsche writes:

> [T]he state tells lies in all the tongues of good and evil; and whatever it says it lies—and whatever it has it has stolen. Everything about it is false; it bites with stolen teeth, and bites easily. Even its entrails are false. Confusion of tongues of good and evil: this sign I give you as a sign of the state. Verily, this sign signifies the will to death. Verily, it beckons to the preachers of death.[2]

Nietzsche asserts for several reasons that the state is a lie. First, the state is a sort of congealed morality, a permanent token of the fact that we despise the way things are. But even on that level, it is a sheer hypocrisy: the modern state is always instituting "reforms," vowing to make over this or that "sector of society," but is itself the sector of society least liable to reform.

Of course, and as Nietzsche saw very clearly in *The Genealogy of Morals*, the state is in the business of imposing its transformations on people by the very means that it condemns as immoral. It prohibits theft, and enforces this prohibition under the auspices of taxation, that is, by theft. It kills to enforce the prohibition of killing, and so forth. Thoreau writes:

> It is not to be forgotten, that while the law holds fast the thief and murderer, it lets itself go loose. When I have not paid the tax which the state demanded for that protection which I did not want, itself has robbed me; when I asserted the liberty it presumed to declare, itself has imprisoned me. (*A Week*, 105)

Such truths are too commonplace really to need any reiteration, though Thoreau's placement of them into personal experience is felicitous.

The real problem of the state, however, lies at a different level; we ought to be ontologically anxious about the state. For the state is an abstraction, and it proceeds insofar as people are ready to treat one another as abstractions. It is a huge fantastic mechanism for the denial of the truth of the people it "rules." The state is, in the final analysis, merely an attempt to convert human beings into concepts: into "king" and "subject," "minister" and "criminal," "agency" and "voter," and so forth. Thoreau puts it like this:

> [The officer of the state], as a living man, may have human virtues and a thought in his brain, but as the

tool of an institution, a jailer or constable it may be, he is not a whit superior to his prison key or his staff. Herein is the tragedy; that men doing outrage to their proper natures, even those called wise and good, lend themselves to perform the office of inferior and brutal ones. Hence come war and slavery in; and what else may not come in through this opening? (*A Week*, 107)

The engineering of individual human beings into jailers is fictional; the engineering of masses of men into institutions is, as well. But the war and brutality that these people perpetuate when they have been, in the words of Kierkegaard, "fantastically made over" are all too actual.

A state may be thought of in two general ways: as an institutional structure and a structure of texts (constitutions, laws, regulations), or as persons who assert and partially enforce a monopoly of violence over a certain region. On the first construal, the laws and institutions in question may be held to arise as the result of, say, a social contract or a class struggle. The state so described may be held to have as a purpose the preservation of rights or the maintenance or destruction of class ascendancy. This is the way the state is described by, for example, Locke, Marx, and Rawls. All these thinkers view the state as an "abstract" object. Government on these views is a *structure* in which individuals occupy various places.

This view, I think, represents a fundamental fallacy; it reifies, or rather dereifies, the state into something inhuman, something fantastic. The state thus becomes the ultimate treatment for the fact that we cannot tolerate the reality of other persons: We both make these persons over into concepts and also attempt to control their messy humanity by means of the state. Advocates of this picture of the state sometimes speak of "the rule of law." But laws conceived as texts are incapable of ruling anything or anyone. Laws are, in fact, constituted as laws by certain human relations, relations of authority and obedience. And institutions consist of the human beings who compose them and of the human results they procure. I shall term the visions that deploy the notion of the state as law and institution the "cult" of the state; they have in common the view that government is a textual or institutional entity which stands above particular human beings and restrains them in various ways. I assert that the second view—the view that the state is a group of people who claim and, in part, exercise a monopoly of violence—is merely an accurate description of the reality of the state. The state is a street gang. So I interpret Thoreau and Nietzsche's claims about the unreality of the state as saying that the state does not exist *as it wants to understand itself*; it does not exist as a structure of laws and institutions. Laws and institutions are elaborate blinds, designed to camouflage the jackboot on your throat.

I am not going to attempt to argue here that the cult of the state is false. Rather, I am going to attempt, with the help of Vaclav Havel's political essays reprinted in the volume *Living in Truth*, to show that it is pernicious, that the results of taking it seriously are disastrous. Certainly, they are disastrous if we take seriously the values of truth and love as I have tried to develop them.

In every state, individuals exercise and obey authority which ultimately rests on violence. This by itself does not show that state power is never "legitimate"; there are, after all, legitimate uses of violence. And of course, I, by my own lights, am probably not going to be able to condemn things on the basis of their illegitimacy; it's their unreality that concerns me. What I want to discuss, then, is the way the state "apparatus" attempts to conceal its own origins and the sources of its power and how the people who live within the state attempt to "rationalize" the authority of the state, to think of it as something impersonal and inevitable. The problem here, in other words, is not about the reality of the situation; it is about people's account to themselves of that reality. People relieve the political authorities of the responsibility for their exercise of authority, and they relieve themselves of responsibility for obedience. Responsibility is one of the central notions in Havel's political philosophy. The word, of course, has a very moralistic ring, and brings into play an entire system of moral evaluation—blame and praise accruing to actions accomplished freely and so on— of which I want no part. But what I mean by "responsibility" here is something more mundane: To act in one's capacity as a jailer, for instance, is simply to deny that one's actions *are* one's actions, to seek to mitigate the assignment of one's actions to oneself. To be "responsible" for one's actions in this sense is simply to *be* the one who performs them. The state's account of itself is a huge machinery for accomplishing this mitigation; the history of the state is a history of attempting to assign one's own actions to something else, preferably something that does not exist at all: The Majesty of the Law, for example.

Havel writes, profoundly:

> We could say that, for all the complex historical detours, the origin of the modern state and modern political power may be sought . . . in a moment when human reason begins to "free" itself from the human being as such, from his personal experience, personal conscience and personal responsibility.[3]

Havel claims that this attempt to "free" reason and power from their origins in human beings and release them into a realm in which they operate independently of any particular persons is "the essential trait of modern civilization," though it has its clearest manifestation in Stalinist systems. As Havel puts it in "An Anatomy of Reticence," in all systems that embody a cult, Stalinist or not, "the project for a better world ceases to be an expression of man's responsibility and begins, on the contrary, to appropriate his responsibility and identity, . . . the abstraction ceases to belong to him and he instead begins to belong to it" (175).

The cult of the state has its most extreme philosophical proponent in Hegel. Hegel declared that "the state must be treated as a great architectonic structure, as a hieroglyph of the reason which reveals itself in actuality."[4] This is an extremely succinct formulation of the nature of the state according to those that make of it a cult. The state, on this view, is an "architectonic structure" rather than a bunch of people, an abstract character or hieroglyph rather than a concrete inscription. Both these claims will prove important in what follows. But for now we can note that Hegel gives a very clear version of the picture of the state as a depersonalized power. Here the state is monstrously bloated into the necessary unfolding of reason and so forth, having nothing to do with individual decisions and imaginatively releasing everyone from concrete involvement. Kierkegaard wrote that such philosophical systems as Hegel's treat the knowing subject in such a way that "it becomes something that no existing human being ever was or can be."[5] The cult of the state in all its forms makes the state something no group of human beings ever was or can be.

The essays of Havel under consideration here were written under very particular pressures and addressed to very particular circumstances. They were written by a persecuted intellectual (a "dissident") to elucidate and attack the sources of his persecution. But Havel attempts to reach some general conclusions from his particular circumstances, and I will pursue the wider implications of his claims.

Havel held that the sort of system he faced in Czechoslovakia, a system in which the government assumes the role of social engineer to an extreme degree, was historically unprecedented. For this reason, he coins a new term for such systems: He calls them "post-totalitarian." He sharply differentiates such systems from simple totalitarian arrangements or "classical dictatorships," which rely on the more or less naked exercise of power by a

single person or a small group of people. It is in a classical
dictatorship that the picture of government as a street
gang is most obviously appropriate. In a post-totalitarian
system, however, the use of power is hardly ever "naked."
Rather, each such society has been "penetrated by a net-
work of manipulatory instruments" ("The Power of the Powerless," 37): an ideology that answers all political questions and a system of surveillance and extralegal
punishments for expressions of dissent (including loss of
livelihood, of one's children's educational opportunities,
and so forth).

The post-totalitarian system, Havel says, deploys a
"precise, logically structured, generally comprehensible
ideology that, in its elaborateness and completeness, is
almost a secularized religion" (38). In such a system, Marxist ideology is the fundamental instrument for the depersonalization of power. There is one salient feature of this
ideology that dwarfs all others: It is manifestly and
obscenely false to the situation at hand. It is a system of
lies that people are forced to pretend to acknowledge as
the truth:

> Government by bureaucracy is called popular gov-
> ernment; the working class is enslaved in the name of
> the working class; the complete degradation of the
> individual is presented as his or her ultimate libera-
> tion; depriving people of information is called making
> it available; the use of power to manipulate is called
> the control of power, and the arbitrary use of power is
> called observing the legal code; the repression of cul-
> ture is called its development; the expansion of impe-
> rial influence is presented as support for the
> oppressed; the lack of free expression becomes the
> highest form of freedom; farcical elections become the
> highest form of democracy; banning independent
> thought becomes the most scientific of world views;
> military occupation becomes fraternal assistance.

Because the regime is captive to its own lies, it must falsify everything. It falsifies the past. It falsifies the present, and it falsifies the future. It falsifies statistics. It pretends not to possess an omnipotent and unprincipled police apparatus. It pretends to respect human rights. It pretends to persecute no one. It pretends to fear nothing. It pretends to pretend nothing. (44–45)

The state as a system of laws and institutions only exists in the sense that people pretend or come to believe that it exists. It is no accident that, in its ultimate expression—the post-totalitarian system—the state perpetuates an incredibly elaborate system of lies about everything. But the system that deploys this vast structure of detailed lies about itself, this ideology, can perpetuate itself through that ideology even if *no one* believes its lies (though it is possible that some people may well come to believe them). It is not necessary for the party chairman to believe the ideology he administers. It is not necessary for those who administer the ideology for him (the secret police and so forth) to believe it. And it is not necessary for the people in general, on whom the ideology is administered, to believe it. All that is required is for each of these people to fulfill outwardly the role that ideology prescribes, to act *as if* he or she believed it.[6]

Thus the system demands not commitment but hypocrisy. In Havel's famous example, a greengrocer posts a sign that says "Workers of the World Unite!" in his window. This is not an expression of genuine commitment to the state and its ideology on the part of the grocer, nor does anyone take it to be. Rather, it is an expression of the fact that the grocer does not place himself outside the system, and thus that he deserves to remain unmolested.

Power in such a society gradually becomes more and more abstract; it seems to be invested not in individuals but in the ideology and its institutions:

> Power gradually draws closer to ideology than it does
> to reality; it draws its strength from theory and
> becomes entirely dependent on it. This inevitably
> leads, of course, to a paradoxical result: rather than
> theory, or rather ideology, serving power, power begins
> to serve ideology. It is as though ideology had appro-
> priated power from power, as though it had become
> dictator itself. It thus appears that theory itself, ritual
> itself, ideology itself, makes decisions that affect peo-
> ple, and not the other way around. (47)

One rises to power in such a system, Havel says, by "allowing oneself to be borne aloft" by ideology.

Now I suggest that this investment of ideology with a
mythic momentum of its own, this apparent dictatorship
by words rather than human beings, derives directly from
taking the model of government as text and institution, as
abstract object, with an unprecedented seriousness. A
post-totalitarian system is a system in which the power of
human beings over human beings is disowned and mythologically reified into an abstract, independently existing
object. This is not to say that no one actually wields power
in such a system. But no one in such a system *acknowledges* responsibility, and elaborate mechanisms are developed to allow their responsibility to remain unacknowl-
edged. For this reason, Havel, in the "Letter to Dr. Gustav
Husak," refers to the post-totalitarian system as "entropic";
it is opposed to life, which seeks spontaneity and variety in
individual manifestations. This is Nietzsche's fundamental
insight about the state as well: that at the heart of its false
self-understanding there is a will to death. The state, in
this sense, is life and power that have turned against life
and that express their hatred for life in the most literal
possible terms: by eradicating differences—finally, by eradicating people.

No one in a post-totalitarian system seems to bear any
personal responsibility for anything. The "responsibility"

that exists is supposed to be entirely structural, ideological; individuals, from Husak to the greengrocer, merely perform the structurally prescribed functions. They are, or rather are fantasized as being, mere locations in the structure, placeholders of the ideology. The state is, to repeat, apparently not a group or even a system of human beings but an independently existing abstract entity. In fact, the very same structure (with minor variations) can be repeatedly instantiated: in Hungary, Poland, and so forth. (And such structures are still in place in China, North Korea, Cuba, and other countries, as well as in the democratic West insofar as it, too, makes a cult of the state.)

The state is, in this sense, like a text: an abstract structure that can appear in many particular inscriptions. The text "itself" is not any of its particular inscriptions; it can be repeated *ad infinitum* using different materials. Likewise, the state itself is not any particular group of individuals; it does not consist of anyone. It is a dictatorial structure in which people enact various roles, not a dictatorship of individuals (a "classical dictatorship").

This brings us to the central concepts of Havel's political philosophy, which are also central to the postethical "ethics" I have been constructing: living within a lie and living in truth. On a Marxist conception of the state, according to which the state is always the instrument of the oppression of one class by another, a society can be fairly neatly divided into oppressor (the bourgeoisie, say, or the feudal lord) and oppressed (the proletariat, the serf). But this is not the case in a post-totalitarian system:

> Here, by the way, is one of the most important differences between the post-totalitarian system and classical dictatorships, in which the line of conflict can still be drawn according to social class. In the post-totalitarian system, this line runs *de facto* through each person, for everyone in his or her own way is both a victim and supporter of the system. (53)

Each person, that is to say, "lives within the lie," fulfills her function within the structure, acts as if she believes the ideology. Such systems, and *all* systems, insofar as they are "systems," have the function of turning people into place holders within the structure. This compromises the experiences they have of themselves as real, as it compromises their ability to say what is true. Of course, nothing can actually compromise the reality of persons except by literally killing them; but people can be made to experience life as if they were already dead, to experience themselves as abstractions rather than organisms.

So, in a certain sense and to a certain degree, post-totalitarian systems succeed in carrying out Marx's goal of ending class struggle. The fundamental conflict in a post-totalitarian system is not between some persons who are oppressors and some people who are oppressed. Rather, each person is *both* oppressor and oppressed; he is divided from himself into both "a victim and supporter of the system." Thus, the system is "alienating" in Marx's sense but in a way Marx could not have anticipated. Havel terms the condition of this alienation "auto-totality." Auto-totality consists in the oppression of each person by himself, in the fact that the lines of power run through each person.

This provokes for each person in such a society an existential crisis, a division within the self that compromises each person's experience of herself as real. Havel's solution to this crisis is simple, though unutterably difficult: The only possible way to end the internal division is to enact its conflation externally. Each person must refuse to enact her ritual role within the structure. This solution is precisely what we should expect, for again one finds one's truth by entering into relations. One's truth is one's situation. People must begin to "live in truth," and live it in the world, or else even a change in systems will not solve their existential problem. The greengrocer must refuse to post the sign. The only effective attack on a system that seeks to divide each person from himself, to provoke an existential crisis within each person, is personal existential transformation through external enactment of authenticity. Havel, that is, issues a call to truth.

That is why Havel does not seek to replace the ruling ideology with a new ideology, why (at this stage of his career, at any rate), he refuses to talk, say, about instituting liberal democracy or revising the constitution. A new ideology might do something to ameliorate conditions, might make the system somewhat less indifferent to individual needs. But the fundamental problem with the ideology of the post-totalitarian system is not *what* it says. After all, it talks about liberation, equality, freedom of expression, free elections. The problem, rather, lies in *how* the ideology is employed. Almost any systematic and more or less consistent body of political doctrine could perform the same function. The Czechoslovak government could have operated more or less just as well with the U.S. Constitution or the Magna Charta. The text may serve as a trace of people's resolution, or, as here, of their hypocrisy, but it is itself no wielder of power.

What is needed is not a new political program but a new way of thinking about one's life and one's role with regard to the state. Havel writes:

> No matter how beautiful an alternative political model may be, it can no longer speak to the 'hidden sphere,' inspire people and society, call for real political ferment. . . . People who live in a post-totalitarian system know only too well that the question of whether one or several political parties are in power, and how these parties define or label themselves, is of far less importance than the question of whether or not it is possible to live like a human being. . . . A genuine, profound, and lasting change for the better . . . can no longer result from the victory . . . of any particular traditional political conception. More than ever before, such a

change will have to derive from the fundamental reconstitution of the position of people in the world, their relationship to themselves and each other, and to the universe. . . . A better system will not automatically ensure a better life. In fact the opposite is true: only by creating a better life can a better system be developed. (69–71)

It is not hard to see why a dissident in a post-totalitarian system would be leery of *all* ideology, of *all* potential programs; he sees how easily any such program can be converted into lies, how easily the claim that the ideals of the program have been fulfilled can be substituted for their actual fulfillment. Or rather, such a person smells lies as soon as any ideology starts to be enunciated. The most extreme moralism—that is, the most extreme negation of reality—always takes an ideological form, and expresses itself, perhaps, as a utopian scheme. This is as true of Plato as it is of Marx. What is expressed in the construction of a utopia is a hatred of social reality *in toto*, a resolution no longer to tolerate anything social insofar as it is presently real. (It is worth noting that this act of negation takes in Marx a "scientific" form.) And every statist ideology participates in this hatred of the real to one degree or another, and can lead back to the depersonalization of power and the cult of the state.

The sort of crisis that Havel discusses is, thus, inherent in any state of which there is a cult. Any state that is thought of as a mere structure, an abstract system, a group of laws and institutions, and so forth, rather than as a group of human beings, has already imaginatively detached itself from reality. For such a conception of the state destroys the sense of reality in its "components." People experience themselves as if they were enacting roles and fulfilling functions rather than living lives. The cult of the state relies on a lie about the ontology of the state, and always carries within it the potential to make people live within the lie. Alternative ideologies of the state are only alternative ways of arranging lies: An ideology prescribes a structure, and it describes places within the structure to be assumed by people, but it does not, cannot, describe *people*. Every ideology of the state is a permutation of the cult of the state, and relies on abstraction from actual persons and concrete conditions. Thus it seeks to deprive people of their authenticity.

Indeed, Havel does not confine his point to post-totalitarian systems, which simply take to extreme lengths the autototality and individual inauthenticity inherent in political ideology:

> And in the end, is not the greyness and emptiness of life in the post-totalitarian system only an inflated caricature of modern life in general? And do we not in fact stand (although in the external measures of civilization, we are far behind) as a kind of warning to the West, revealing its own latent tendencies? (54)

Some ideologies and some political programs are better than others, and some systems do a better job of living up to their ideologies than do others. But every ideology harbors the potential for abuse; every political "program" has already been detached from reality and started to float free of actual conditions. Just as is every conceptuality, but to a particularly virulent degree, every political ideology is an expression of implacable hatred of the world, a fear and loathing that is, in the case of ideology, so thorough that it seeks a total transformation of the social. But total transformation is impossible; the world and the persons in it are jagged, recalcitrant. So the ideology simply floats free of the real and becomes a creature of imagination, compensates itself as fiction for what it can never have as fact.

As with any philosophical or conceptual system, people will wind up simply asserting the truth of an ideology as a compensation for their inability to tolerate its falsity, preferring it to the actual. In fact, American ideology already does this to a remarkable extent; politicians "wrap themselves in the flag" and talk of liberty and equality and free enterprise while quietly beefing up the apparatus of state-supported monopoly capital and automatism.

II.

It will hardly come as a surprise that Havel offers no political program. He calls, rather, for "anti-political politics," "politics 'from below.' Politics of man, not of apparatus. Politics growing from the heart, not a thesis" (157). He could hardly offer an alternative ideology and remain consistent. Rather, he proceeds from the opposite direction: Again, a better life for particular people will give rise to a better "system," not vice versa. No concrete change has ever been achieved by designing a set of concepts and then slapping them on the real. The real slaps back, and harder. All debates about what government system is "best" are absurd: as if we could sit back and simply impose on the real whatever structure our whim might prescribe. That is a delusion of grandeur, or, again, a symptom of the Western philosophical problem: What is a mind doing in a world? The only answer we seem to give is, It's here to *take over*. But a mind is supposed to be a nonphysical object, and a nonphysical object can have no physical effects. So this tiny "mind" rages at its impotence, or compensates itself for its impotence in fact by omnipotence in imagination, until we are having a truly idiotic dialogue about how to arrange our culture. Meanwhile, of course, our culture is arranging us. The fact is, we cannot remake each other. But we *could* remake each other if we could turn each other into concepts, into roles, blanks, ideas. And so we . . . pretend to. Meanwhile, what is actually going on is that people are killing people, people are shutting people up, people are taking other people's stuff. But "we" aren't doing this, because "we" are just concepts: citizens, congressmen, and so forth.

People can achieve a life in truth only by their own efforts at transformation or, better, by their own attempts at "realization," since what they must do is come to see that they are already, in truth, living. A "better life" that is imposed on people is initially a contentless burden and finally a patent lie. Havel writes that "the issue is the rehabilitation of values like trust, openness, responsibility, solidarity, love" (118). Such values cannot be politically created. The most elaborate mechanisms for the repression of hate, irresponsibility, mistrust serve only to exacerbate the conditions they address; where political systems are not irrelevant to the love and trust of people who live under them, they are inimical to these goals. Love cannot be legislated (obviously), because love and legislation are very different in that love is real and legislation is not. Legislation is lies, whereas love is always an experience of and acknowledgment of reality. Love could be enacted by government decree (and we of the West are at times close to this lunatic pass, as when the government threatens to legislate away violence on television because of its effects on our affections), but the only instruments at the command of government to enforce love are guns, clubs, jails, and so forth.

In the 1984 essay "Six Asides about Culture," Havel discusses the situation of the arts in post-totalitarian Czechoslovakia, and develops the notion of parallel (dissident) culture that he puts forward in "The Power of the Powerless." He responds to critics of the parallel culture in emigré groups who suggest that the nonofficial arts community is not sufficiently programmatic, that it does not provide a political alternative to the state. But Havel argues that people defined as a group merely by their exclusion *could* not have a particular ideology: "They can never agree on a common programme because the only thing they have in common (which is why they found themselves under the common umbrella in the first place) is their diversity and insistence on being just what they are" (128). This is precisely what constitutes parallel culture as a genuine alternative to the official structures: The participants in the culture possess and encourage in one another the diversity that Havel associates with life. He continues: "If, in spite of everything, they were to agree [on] a common programme, it would be the saddest outcome of all: one uniform confronting another." And several pages later, he adds: "The essence of the conflict . . . is not a confrontation between two ideologies (for instance a socialist with a liberal one) but a clash between an anonymous, soulless, immobile, and paralyzing ('entropic') power, and life, humanity, being in its mystery" (133). Or, to put it another way, the confrontation is between lies and reality. So the parallel culture is open-ended, voluntary, and tolerant of great differences. It is revealing that, in "The Power of the Powerless," Havel suggests that the "parallel polis" might be a model for an alternative political organization for the nation, or, rather, for an alternative to political organization for the nation.

The problem confronting people in post-totalitarian states—and, in fact, confronting all of us—cannot be framed in terms of rival ideological visions. For example, the question of whether we ought to prefer socialism or capitalism is by now an *empty* question, a question merely about which form of autototality is preferable. And it was always an empty question in that the world never arranged itself according to our preferences. We must work, rather, to confront autototality in all its forms. Havel says that the question about whether socialism or capitalism is preferable

gives me a sense of emerging from the depths of the last century. It seems to me that these thoroughly ideological and often semantically confused categories have long since been beside the point. The question is wholly other, deeper, and equally relevant to all; whether we shall, by whatever means, succeed in

reconstituting the natural world as the true terrain of
politics, rehabilitating the personal experience of
human beings as the initial measure of things . . . in
making human community meaningful, in returning
content to human speaking, in reconstituting, as the
focus of all social action, the autonomous, integral,
and dignified human I. (149–50)

The choice is thus not between this or that form of political
organization, or between a command or a market econ-
omy, but between self-division and self-oppression by auto-
totality and a Kierkegaardian transformation toward the
subjective and the infinite.

Here is Havel's conception of the "post-democratic"
politics he endorses:

There can and must be structures that are open,
dynamic, and small; beyond a certain point, human
ties like personal trust and personal responsibility
cannot work. There must be structures that in principle place no limits on the genesis of different structures. Any accumulation of power whatsoever (one of
the characteristics of automatism) should be profoundly alien to it. They would be structures not in
the sense of organizations and institutions, but like a
community. . . . Rather than a strategic agglomera-
tion of formalized organization, it is better to have
organizations springing up *ad hoc*, infused with enthu-
siasm for a particular purpose and disappearing when
that purpose has been achieved. (118)

These claims sound, in a way, like the ideology they are
designed to reject: There should be organizations of this
kind, and so on. But the point is, Havel is willing to simply
wait and see what happens: his "living in truth" is, in that
sense, Heideggerian: It resolves to let people be. This, I suggest, is a form of anarchism, specifically a form of anar-

cho-syndicalism. It does not preclude social arrangements of various kinds but would have them be small scale, voluntary, ephemeral. The French syndicalist Fernand Pelloutier wrote that a syndicate is "an association you are free to enter or leave, without a president."[7] One can have a syndicate of intellectuals or artists (and not only, as on the traditional syndicalist conception, workers), in this sense.

The notion of community is to be contrasted with the *mythos* of the state. Mythologically, to repeat, the state consists of texts (constitutions, laws), institutions, and so forth rather than of human beings. It is as if you could drop a neutron bomb on the state and it would live on; the state in this sense is, in Havel's terms, "anonymous, impersonal and inhuman power—the power of ideologies, systems, *apparat*, bureaucracy, artificial languages and political slogans" (153). A community, on the other hand, is just some persons in a certain equilibrium. A community consists without remainder of its members. And the actuality of the state is almost as inimical to community as the mythology of the state. In reality, the state is based on violence by certain persons against others, the enforcement by violence of strictures on violence, and so forth. But this is incompatible with community; to the extent that organization is imposed, it cannot be communitarian. I cannot force you to become part of a community, to love or trust or feel solidarity with its members. You make yourself part of a community, more or less consciously, and your continued participation is optional.

If it is true that Havel is (or, at any rate, at one time was) an anarcho-syndicalist, it might be asserted that he *does* have a political program. But anarchists traditionally have been extremely reticent to describe their envisioned future—or, for that matter, to envision it. For example, Emma Goldman wrote:

I believe that Anarchism cannot consistently impose an iron-clad program or method on the future. . . .

Anarchism, as I understand it, leaves posterity free to develop its own particular systems, in harmony with its needs. Our most vivid imagination cannot foresee the potentialities of a race set free from external restraints. How, then, can any one assume to map out a line of conduct for those to come? We, who must pay dearly for every breath of pure, fresh air, must guard against the tendency to fetter the future.[8]

Havel's "program," such as it is, is precisely to let people develop their own programs, to come to whatever voluntary arrangements seem best to them, to allow people to be. That is a way of living in truth and of encouraging people to come to live in truth.

Nevertheless, in various ways, Havel's position is distinct from traditional anarchism. In particular, most traditional anarchists, from Godwin on, hold the view that the natural benevolent propensities of people are distorted by the state. It is interesting to note that, in this respect, the traditional anarchist view is itself a version of the cult of the state, though bent on sacrilege. It fails to recognize that the state is simply a bunch of people, on the whole neither better nor worse than average. On the traditional anarchist view, the state is a monstrous distortive *mechanism*. As on the statist conception, it is held to be an abstract force, but it is claimed that this force pulls people apart rather than joining them together.

Havel does not share the traditional anarchist's view that the elimination of the state is itself a panacea, that the elimination of the state will allow people's benevolence to find expression. People obviously have the potential to live within the lie, to sacrifice their integrity for material comfort; people participate in their own oppression. But, by the same token, there is in each person a yearning toward integrity, reality, and solidarity; each person harbors the potential to live in truth. Thus, no particular political action, even the dismantling of the state, can cure what ails us. It is perfectly possible to live a lie in the absence of the state. The state, however, does raise rather obvious barriers to living in truth, and the cult of the state systematizes these barriers. But coming to live in truth is something each person must do for herself, and it is only by individual people coming to live in truth that a radical decentralization of authority could be achieved and could have meaning. Again, the political transformation has to come from below, in a form that inconspicuously swamps authority and renders it useless. The society will be transformed not by the intelligentsia leading a revolutionary army but by greengrocers truly greengrocering. This should not, however, be mistaken for quietism: Public heroism will be demanded in order to point out and resist the system's lies.

But the fundamental reason I would like to read Havel as an anarchist is this: There can be no question of *forcing* or *constraining* people to live in truth. As Kierkegaard might have said, that is a task to occupy an entire life and which each person faces for himself, not as a place holder in the system, as a citizen, but as a concrete individual. The problem with the state is, in sum, this: that it is an attempt to treat the people who compose it as fantastic abstractions, an attempt to fantastically make them over into "roles." It will make you into an abstraction, and there is only one way to accomplish this: by violence. The state, thus, is both itself a lie and a maker of lies: It seeks to make everything false by departicularizing it; hence, it is a philosophy and a technology, an instrument of power and of death.

5

POWER, OPENNESS, EARTH

This chapter is about the way of life of the Lakota Sioux. Lakota culture is useful for present purposes because there is so much primary and dictated source material. I make use here of five works. First, there are the classic books dictated by Black Elk, a Sioux holy man who lived through Little Big Horn and Wounded Knee: *Black Elk Speaks* (an autobiography) and *The Sacred Pipe* (a description of Oglala ceremonial). Based to one extent or another on these two books and on oral traditions involving Black Elk, a number of books have appeared describing Sioux religion from the inside; the three I discuss below are the wonderful *Lame Deer Seeker of Visions*, by John (Fire) Lame Deer and Richard Erdoes, Ed McGaa's *Mother Earth Spirituality*, and *Fools Crow: Wisdom and Power*, by Thomas Mails in dialogue with Fools Crow.

I.

I will contrast the Lakota material to the interlocking notions of power, comprehension, and representation as these appear in Western culture or, at any rate, in Western intellectual life. As I have discussed, we can detach ourselves from the world in a number of ways. One way is "spiritual"; we make ourselves over into ghosts. Though the Enlightenment eventually threw that view into question in the West, eventually led us to a "mechanistic" approach to the world and ourselves, it, too, contained a way out of situation.

World-affirmation always appears in stunted form (and I am sure it so appears here). No affirmation is without soil; no affirmation is pure or perfect or total. That is an indication of the poignancy with which reality confronts us, its ubiquity and mercilessness. Nietzsche, for instance, affirmed, but also engaged in the horrible fantasy of the "overman"; he wanted out of humanity, which he found for the most part despicable. (That, of course, raises the question of Nietzsche's attitude toward . . . himself.) Emerson loved the world, but viewed it as an emanation of the invisible realm of Spirit. Santayana elucidated our commitment, as animals, to actuality, but still thought the world concealed itself behind a veil of essences and intuitions.

Science has embedded us in the real, shown us how to understand ourselves as organisms, and so forth. It has reduced our pretensions to a "higher" sort of being, has "killed God." But the structure of science as an inquiry into the world is, first of all, articulated by an empiricist epistemology. Classical empiricism told us that we experienced the world only in, or even only as, a series of ideas or mental images. Thus, science has always conceived its project in terms derived from depiction: It has always conceived its project as the construction of adequate representations (or, alternately, descriptions). Representation as conceived in the West, I have claimed, detaches the person who experiences it from the thing that is represented and empowers one over it. In this sense, to "study" something is to lose it. The closer you get to an accurate representation of it—the more, for example, you magnify it using instruments with the object of getting a good picture of what it is like—the further it recedes into an aesthetic distance. Thus, any form of scientific inquiry that self-avowedly implicates the scientist in the object of study is held in suspicion; think of the work of Jane Goodall and others with the great apes, or the notion that anthropology is compromised as science by the involvement of the field worker in the target culture (as John Neihardt [who worked with Black Elk], Erdoes, and Mails are perhaps implicated in the texts I will discuss).

It must be emphasized that if it is, indeed, something real that the scientist studies, then the implication of the scientist in the object of study is always more or less total. One is always implicated in the world, and studying the world entangles one in it more and more. It is precisely that fact that can be forgotten or repressed when the project of science is conceived as the construction of adequate representations. One might go so far as to speculate that science, like religion, is often engaged in precisely as a flight from the world. Only here the direction of flight is more interesting and subtle. For one flies, apparently, precisely *to* the world: to truth, to fact. But when one arrives at these truths and facts, one finds oneself detached from them; one examines them coldly, dispassionately, and so forth; one is engaged in "pure" research. One *finds out about things* in this sense precisely as a way of avoiding engagement with them; one establishes an "impersonal" relationship with the "data." Indeed, the primary test for the quality of an experiment, its reproducibility, is precisely a removal from situation, a disembedding in particularity. The correct result is not the result *I* got on the particular occasion but the result *anyone* would get *in similar circumstances*. Thus, things are valued not as particular objects but as examples of laws and so forth, as "phenomena." If we think about this with regard to psychological methodology, the results can become really horrible. Your marriage, say, becomes a "phenomenon"; its primary use is to show how anyone would act or emote or whatever under similar circumstances. Psychology thus becomes a technical facility for producing persons of certain kinds rather than a way of engaging particular people in their situations. To be a psychologist of that stripe is to flee people by learning more and more about them.

As I've already indicated, the theory of evolution, which, on one level, obviously displays our implication in nature, showing us to be animals, somehow gets worked up into a cute little narrative of ascent; not surprisingly, this ascent culminates in us, who are doing the narrating. Thus, we survey nature not from the heavens but from the heights of nature itself: Nature has been doing its messy work for millions of years for the sake of . . . us. That surely is not itself a scientific result: Any relatively populous species has as good a claim on the evolutionary heights as we, and the world as described in evolutionary biology presents a wild profusion of organisms adapting to a volatile environment rather than a dignified procession from the amoeba to Crispin Sartwell.

Now notice that in the Western tradition (Pythagoras, Plato, Descartes), it is the appearance of thought in nature that is thematized as something that stands in need of explanation. It is thought that separates us from the order of nature or suggests that we are souls, that places us at a distance from the environment. "Science" simply appropriates this "insight" by associating thought with evolutionary ascent. It is *consciousness* that shows man to stand as nature's crowning glory, just as it was, in the end, consciousness that showed us to be made in the image of God or really to be little gods. And it is consciousness, hence, that authorizes our *dominion* over the planet. What distinguishes human from animal consciousness is generalization, abstraction, concept formation, and so forth. Thus, what allows us to detach ourselves from reality in imagination and prospective construction is precisely what shows alternately that we are not of the order of nature, or that we are nature's crowning achievement. That which demonstrates that we cannot tolerate the world and ourselves as part of the world "demonstrates" that we are not *merely* parts of the world but the world's culmination.

This problem is not, I think, overcome in Nietzsche's writings. Not that Nietzsche was scientistic in this sense;

Nietzsche's observations about scientism are among the most trenchant ever produced. But Nietzsche believed that we puny human beings are important because we prepare the way for the overman, the man beyond good and evil, the man of joyous affirmation. *That* would, I guess, be nature's crowning achievement. And Nietzsche sees the deepest expression of life in dominion over the real, power over the world, the will to transformation. There is deep insight in that, and our attempt to exercise power over the real is, indeed, an emerging of the life within us.

Notice, though, that power, like representation, distances. And power often, or perhaps in human culture always, proceeds precisely *through* representation, so that to represent a culture in ethnography (or as I am about to do to the Lakota) is to *appropriate* it, to turn it into an expression of your power by displaying your *comprehension* of it. To do this retrospectively is to engage in science; to do it prospectively is to engage in political ideology. And in this way, the representation of the world is directly, and not accidentally, linked to the exercise of power over the world that is embodied in technology, as Heidegger argued. To have comprehended the world in a scientific representation is already to have made it available for use, to have brought it under your control. You have already, in trying to construct an adequate representation, expressed your *right*, not to say your resolution, to make use of what is represented. And, of course, science is connected with use in exactly this way, so that to *understand* the atom is to release its potential power, or rather, to release ourselves into the use of that power. In this sense there is no "pure" research; every accurate result of research is a making available of things as instruments of human power. And one sees precisely the same move in the "human sciences" and their expression in ideology.

To exercise power over something is to declare one's autonomy from it; the thing over which power is exercised may depend upon the one who exercises power, but (apparently) the one who exercises power does not depend upon the object over which power is exercised. Thus, to potentiate power over the world through science and put it to work through technology is to declare that we do not need the world, that we stand outside it as we reign over it. In this sense, science separates us from the world every bit as much as, say, Christianity. Indeed, as Nietzsche noticed, science is perhaps simply the latest permutation of Christianity. Regarding the world as an object over which power can be exercised is itself implicated, first, in the classical structure of representation; second, in the construction of ethical values; and third, in the cult of the state. One exercises power, that is, to convert what is into what ought to be. It was Nietzsche's great realization that every *making of values* is drawn from the deep wellspring of a will to power. But he failed, I think, to notice that the deepest expression of affirmation yields, finally, an ability to *let go* of power or of the pretension to power.

Whenever I am experiencing myself as powerful, I am experiencing myself as something with both the right and the ability to remake things as they ought to be, and I am, hence, experiencing things as though they can or must be remade. For power, as we know, often emerges from hatred; hatred is empowering. Nietzsche, for one, is great in his hatreds, as he is great in his loves. And power, especially power that emerges from hatred, is, as we also know, often, or rather always, fraudulent.

Take, for example, political and technological power. The exercise of political power is, no doubt, an expression of the life within those who exercise it. We create, say, a post-totalitarian regime as the expression of life, and then we use it precisely to eradicate any signs of life we may detect. When the life within me expresses itself as political power, it has turned into something hostile, precisely, to life. Life becomes celebratory when it makes things around it alive, lets things live, not when it makes things dead. But the expression of life as power is a long killing. The "powerful personality" who gathers around himself a group of disciples or the man who dominates or enslaves his family expresses the life within him at the expense of the life out there. Or rather, he uses the life around him to feed his power—he *consumes* life. When two men meet, they often do a little power dance: Who is the stronger, who the smarter? And who will dominate the other? If you acknowledge that I am more powerful than you, you invite me to *appropriate* your power, to suck the life out of you, to turn your own life against itself.

We live this way with regard to the planet as a whole. Our exercise of "dominion" over the planet, established by our status as thinking things—that is, as beings capable of representation—is a destruction of the life of the planet. We quite literally use its life to feed ourselves; we kill it in an expression of our aliveness. This is precisely the distinctive aspect of "technological thinking": We distance ourselves from the world as an expression of knowledge and power; we revel in our power over the world, but this power is a killing. We have learned, that is, to hate life, for a life that seeks to express itself in power over the world is life that has learned to hate life. But how can one learn to hate life without learning also to hate being alive? The exercise of power—personal, political, marital, technological—is, finally, world-hatred in its most definite form; it is a "making of values"; it is life that hates life and, hence, itself as a living thing: life as a *parasite*, living on the energy of other lives, life as destruction. Power, hence, is for us the greatest danger, the greatest temptation, the deepest expression of our hatred and self-hatred. It is the instrument by which we deaden one another and ourselves. In the final accounting, power as it is conceived in the West is delusion and death: delusion because it holds us away in imagination from that over which we exercise power (we kill Jews, say, to emphasize the fact that *we are not Jews*), and death because it sucks the life out of its object and, finally, out of itself.

I suppose, with Nietzsche, that the first arena of the exercise of power is within the self. One has to come to be powerful over oneself if one is to subdue the other. To take command of others, one must first have taken command of oneself. But notice how odd it is to "take command of oneself," as if one were two different things: one thing which exercises power (a "will") and one thing over which power is exercised (*what is that?*). Thus, to exercise power over oneself is to be the parasite of oneself, to live at the expense of *one's own* life. To exercise "will power" is to impoverish and dehumanize oneself. And every exercise of power in the external world presupposes that one is willing also to exercise power over oneself, which entails, of course, that one is also one's own victim, that one oppresses oneself. Thus, the will to command oneself is also always simultaneously the will *to be commanded.* Self-command is self-enslavement. Thoreau writes: "It is hard to have a southern overseer; it is worse to have a northern one; but worst of all when you are the slave-driver of yourself."[1]

Thus, "powerful" men—dictators, CEOs, and so forth—slowly become "inhuman"; every exercise of power over others originates in self-control. Indeed, this sets in motion a vicious circle in which one reduces or appropriates the life within oneself by self-command, and then seeks to make good the deficit by appropriating the life of others, that is, by exercising power externally. One keeps *using people up*, and needs to find new people to "bend to one's will" or simply to kill. Think of Mao, for example, monstrously bloated into a sheer symbol of power: something, finally, that even while it lives has run out of life, even in a culture of hundreds of millions of people. Mao, like Lenin, has the perfect monument: his own corpse, preserved by who knows what necromancy. Such men do not even need to be alive to exercise power; they encorpsed themselves long before they died. That is what fitted them to be "leaders." If you want to know what horror is, think about what that must have been like *from the inside.*

II.

The Lakota tradition, like all traditions, is also stunted in its affirmation of the real. As did Emerson, but with more thoroughness and intensity, the Lakota believe that the physical world is an emanation of the spiritual. The Lakota are, more or less, monotheists who believe that *Wakan Tanka* (the Great Spirit) made and preserves the world. They interpret various physical events as messages or emanations from Wakan Tanka. They believe, too, in a nonphysical human spirit that joins Wakan Tanka at death. Doctrinally, that is, their belief system is quite similar to the Western monotheisms.

The most striking general doctrinal difference between Lakota religion and Western monotheisms (as well as Western scientism) is that the Lakota refuse every attempt to give themselves a special status within nature or a status outside of nature. They do not regard themselves as, say, the guardians of animals but as relatives of animals. They regard themselves as animals, or, as their language reflects, regard animals as persons. They refer to themselves as "two-leggeds" and animals such as buffalo as "four-leggeds," as if the only relevant difference between them were disposition of limbs. (Eagle Man at one point suggests that buffalo, rather than human beings, are created in the image of Wakan Tanka.) And they refer to trees as "tall standing people." Thus they reflect in language their belief in the relatedness of all things on one ontological plane. It is not that human beings are "merely physical"; materialism is not involved at all. Indeed, all things for the traditional Lakota are an emanation of spirit. But that means that people are no more possessed of spirit than are trees. Perhaps what is important in ontologies is not *what sort of entities they recognize* but the ontological *relations* they put into place in their recognition. That is, the fact that human beings and trees are both the same sort of thing is a much deeper aspect of Lakota devotional life than is the detailed doctrine about what sort of thing they are.

But notice the difference here between Lakota attitudes toward nature and that of, say, the Western environmental movement, which has often tried to appropriate Native American beliefs as an "ecologically sound" alternative to Western culture. Western environmentalists, for the most part, are at least as convinced as their enemies that human beings are anomalous in the order of nature. Our problem, on this view, is that human consciousness has given us so much power over the world that we are now responsible for the world's destruction or preservation. We are, again, separated from and placed above the order of nature by our consciousness, our faculty of representation. It is our intelligence, now expressing itself in technological power over the natural world, that sets us up as masters and protectors of nature. For notice that to *protect* something, as to destroy it, is an expression of one's power over that thing. The master not only shackles and exploits the slave, he also protects the slave: The classic argument in favor of slavery is that these dolts, when out of our control, will be defenseless. What stands in need of protection is weak; what offers protection to the weak is strong. We, evolution's crowning achievement, are charged because we are powerful with protecting the earth by our power from our power.

Now we may well have to try to preserve and protect the earth. Otherwise we may destroy ourselves, not to mention the four-leggeds and the tall standing people. But we should not harbor any doubts that to look on the matter this way entails that we believe that we are separated from the order of nature absolutely. Finally, this expresses again how tired we are of sweating and stubbing our toes; we are still, at this late date, making ourselves over into souls. In this empowerment over nature—which, too, issues out of and, in turn, supplements our power over ourselves—we seek to "humanize" nature, whereas we might think instead about letting ourselves become wilder. That is precisely Lame Deer's critique of Western relations to nature:

> You [white folks] have not only altered and malformed your winged and four-legged cousins; you have done it to yourselves. You have changed men into chairmen of boards, into office workers, into time-clock punchers. You have changed your women into housewives, truly fearful creatures. I was once invited to the house of such a one.
>
> "Watch the ashes, don't smoke, you'll stain the curtains. Watch the goldfish bowl, don't lean your head against the wallpaper; your hair may be greasy. Don't spill liquor on that table: it has a delicate finish. You should have wiped your boots; the floor was just varnished. Don't, don't, don't . . ." That is crazy. . . . You live in prisons you have built for yourselves, calling them "homes, offices, factories."[2]

Notice that Lame Deer conceives this not only as a technology of animal husbandry or of the lived environment but above all of the self; one comes, in a process I've discussed, to regard oneself as the role one performs.

Lame Deer continues:

> Americans want everything sanitized. No smells! Not even the good, natural man and woman smell. Take away the smell from under the armpits, from your skin. Rub it out, and then spray or dab some nonhuman odor on yourself. . . . "B.O.," bad breath, "Intimate Female Odor Spray"—I see it all on TV. Soon you'll breed people without body openings. (121)

This is a theme that I will return to at length in the last chapter, but notice here that Lame Deer discusses a technology by which we seek to erase the traces of our embodiment; it is precisely embodiment that "smells bad" to board chairmen and housewives. We homogenize our smells in an attempt to shuck off our bodies and become the pure enactments of our social roles and hence pure spirits. "You are spreading death," says Lame Deer, "buying and selling death. With all your deodorants, you smell of it" (123).

Our entrapment in nature and in our bodies is still embarrassing and inconvenient. And now we feel the trap closing. Or perhaps we now think that mind is itself the problem, which expresses its separation from the earth in pollution and so forth. (A classic philosophical conundrum: how something as ethereal as a mind has effects as concrete as toxic waste.) This presupposes the old dichotomy, though the dichotomy has been rehierarchized. In fact, we turn toward "indigenous peoples" and non-Western cultures precisely because we experience "mind" as a burden; we turn to the "primitive" in a yearning for *body*, or because we suffer from a surfeit of mind, and yearn for a "reunification with nature." The turning toward the primitive always reflects the experience of consciousness as a burden, for primitiveness is associated with unconsciousness, spontaneity, and so forth. (It's obvious that I'm as guilty of this as anyone.) Thus, it is not surprising that we turn toward "primitive" or indigenous peoples when we are trying to figure out how to deal with the problems that consciousness, here expressing itself as technology, has made.

But appropriating such peoples, or consciously seeking an eradication of consciousness, only intensifies consciousness. There can be no *technique* for achieving spontaneity; every application of technique only moves one further from spontaneity. Every attempt to make oneself spontaneous is only, after all, another attempt to control oneself, another exercise of power over the self which is meant, in turn, to effect power over others.

The environmental movement, hence, suggests the further application of power in the service of healing (for all healing is power: is, indeed, perhaps the primordial expression of power), but that movement is still caught up in the dialectic of power. It wants *legislation, regulation*. But though these may help ourselves and other beings to survive, they preserve our view of ourselves, which is at once our deepest self-loathing and our most ostentatious pride, as a bizarre anomaly in nature. They empower us over nature and hence impoverish us, or reduce the life within us. Finally, what is supposed to separate us in the order of nature is "civilization," which is the social expression of mind, the social expression of our powers of generalization and abstraction. And civilization, by the way, simply means *the state*. If you are in doubt about this, look at what the old, politically incorrect anthropology texts called 'civilized': Every people that was in thrall to a state power was *ipso facto* civilized—that is, yanked bodily, or rather spiritually, from the order of nature into the order of culture. Thus, we yearn for a return to no-mind, and this yearning is a yearning for a return to no-civilization. So we try to appropriate (as I am appropriating now) the experience of "uncivilized" persons. But the fact that the environmental movement is still caught up in the notions of mind/soul/civilization in separation from nature is shown by the fact that the instrument of environmental healing is precisely *state power*. Here we put abstractions to work to heal the wounds inflicted by abstractions.

It is disconcerting for some environmentalists intent on appropriating Native American traditions that the Sioux were hunters and warriors. They did not hesitate to kill; in fact, they celebrated killing in various forms. But to kill and gratefully make use of a buffalo is much more to identify oneself as an animal among animals or to identify the buffalo as a soul among souls than is, say, to "preserve" the buffalo as an eponymous representation in a zoo. We preserve the buffalo as a representation, that is, we "picturize" the buffalo, regard the mighty buffalo as "picturesque." Nature is savage. It kills wantonly and randomly. We are part of nature, and we, too, kill wantonly and randomly. But we tell ourselves something else. To love the world and to hate oneself, even for "damaging" the world, is not to love the world. To allow oneself to experience one's worldly situation is the wisdom found in Lakota ceremony. Kill, but kill with joy and reverence, and you will remake our relation to the earth in a much deeper way than by "preservation," which is, to repeat, simply and baldly the exercise of power.

It follows from what I have been saying, I hope, that doctrines (for example, the doctrine that human beings and other things have or are spirits) are of secondary importance in the evaluation of philosophies, religions, cultures. (I admit, first, that I have not drawn this conclusion consistently, that I have been more than willing to condemn, for example, Christianity on doctrinal grounds, and to that extent have falsified it. And second, I admit that I myself substitute doctrines for real openness to the world; indeed, I substitute the doctrine that one should be open to the world for openness to the world. One thing I have noticed is that, for example, people who specialize in ethics are sometimes sociopaths. At any rate, I can turn away from the world by *writing* that we should all turn toward the world.) What matters is not so much what one is saying but how and where one stands: one's posture and location. What matters is not one's philosophical, but one's physical, position.

Every Lakota ceremony puts you in this posture: opening your body to the world's body, celebrating and giving thanks for the world as it is and by means of what nature gives. The fundamental ceremonial act of the Lakota, especially those who take Black Elk's vision seriously, is an acknowledgment of and an opening to the four compass directions, the sky, and the earth. One offers a ceremonial pipe or wotai stone to the six powers, and thus expresses one's veneration of the world. Such an acknowledgment is the beginning and the ending of virtually all

Lakota ceremonies, and carries with it a very elaborate iconography. The pipe ceremony, for instance, that Black Elk embeds in the ceremony for the releasing of a soul that has been dead one year, is typical:

> The helper . . . takes a pinch of the sacred tobacco *kinnikinnik*, and holding it and the stem towards the west, he cries: "With this *wakan* [sacred] tobacco, we place You in the pipe, O winged Power of the west. We are about to send our voices to *Wakan Tanka*, and we wish you to help us! . . . [The celebrant then turns to the north, and says,] O You, Thunder-being, . . . who comes with the purifying winds, and who guards the health of the people; O Baldheaded Eagle of the north, Your wings never tire! There is a place for You too in this pipe. . . . [The celebrant then turns to the east, and says,] O You sacred Being of the place where the sun comes up, who controls knowledge! Yours is the path of the rising sun which brings light into the world. . . . There is a place for you in the pipe. [The celebrant then turns to the south, and says,] You control our life, and the lives of all the peoples of the universe. Everything that moves and all that is will send a voice to *Wakan Tanka*. We have a place for you in the pipe." . . . The stem of the pipe and a pinch of *kinnikinnik* are then held toward the earth. "O You, sacred earth, from whence we have come, You are humble, nourishing all things; we know that you are *wakan* and that with You we are all as relatives. Grandmother and Mother Earth who bear fruit, for you there is a place in this pipe. O Mother, may Your people walk the path of life, facing the strong winds! May we walk firmly upon you! May our steps not falter!"[3]

This ceremony, some form of which is, again, included in virtually every Lakota rite, is, first of all, designed to open

to the world everyone who participates, by an acknowledgment of the four directions and of the earth and the sky. It
associates animals and powers with concrete aspects of
nature in an iconology of the sacred hoop of life. And it
expresses a resolution to hold the earth sacred and walk
upon her with firm steps, even when the wind howls. It is
worth noting that each of the four powers has both a creative and a destructive aspect—the thunderers of the west,
for instance, bring life and also wash it away. But Sioux
religion does not romanticize nature or make it ethical in a
fantasy: It resolves to *love* nature even, or perhaps even
particularly, in its destructive aspect. In that sense, its
love of the earth is a true love.

And it also refrains from making the holy man (*wicasa
wakan*) ethical or unimpaired in a fantasy. In a lovely and
utterly typical passage, Lame Deer says this:

> I believe that being a medicine man, more than any-
> thing else, is a state of mind, a way of looking at and
> understanding this earth, a sense of what it is all
> about. Am I a *wicasa wakan*? I guess so. What else
> can or would I be? Seeing me in my patched-up, faded
> shirt, with my down-at-the-heels cowboy boots, the
> hearing aid whistling in my ear, looking at the flimsy
> shack with its bad-smelling outhouse which I call my
> home—it all doesn't add up to a white man's idea of a
> holy man. You've seen me drunk and broke. You've
> heard me curse or tell a sexy joke. You know I'm not
> better than other men. But I've been up on the hilltop,
> got my vision. (163)

Lame Deer was no ascetic.

It is interesting that the symbolism embodied in
Lakota iconology is a constant acknowledgment of the
dependence of human concepts on nature. Concepts such
as purity, thought, and so forth are understood to be
received from the earth rather than imposed on it intellec-

tually. The order of thought, that is, "globes" rather than creates, constructs, or falsifies the order of the world. Intellect is given to people by the earth. In this aspect, perhaps, Lakota religion stands in contrast to Emerson's thought, with which it is otherwise so allied. Emerson asserted over and over that the order of physical reality reflected the ideal order of thought. But Lakota ceremonial enacts the claim that thought follows the order of nature. That is true, by the way. Understanding is arrived at precisely by an allowance of the world to be. The narratives we make, like everything else we make, are things we do with what we receive from the world.

Black Elk describes the *Hanblecheyapi* ceremony, which is "lamenting" or "crying for a vision" alone on the mountain top, precisely as a long opening of oneself to the world; indeed, the sheer fact that one must *cry* for a vision, that a vision comes to one who *laments*, is important here, for crying and lamenting are ways of making oneself vulnerable, of opening oneself to the world. They are, that is, renunciations of power. In *Black Elk Speaks*, he describes his own crying. He says that, at first, he was only trying to cry, but finally he cried in earnest—indeed, he cried so hard that he thought it might be better if his crying would kill him (*Black Elk Speaks*, 183). The lamenter walks back and forth among the four directions in a cross pattern, opening himself in lament each time to each of the four directions:

> [The lamenter] must always be careful lest distracting thoughts come to him, yet he must be alert to any messenger which the Great Spirit may send him, for these people often come in the form of an animal, even one as seemingly insignificant as a little ant. Perhaps a Spotted Eagle may come to him from the west, or a Black Eagle from the north, or a Bald Eagle from the east, or even the Redheaded woodpecker may come to him from the south. . . . All these people are impor-

tant, for in their own way they are wise and can teach us two-leggeds much if we make ourselves humble before them. (*The Sacred Pipe*, 58)

As Black Elk describes what I suppose is meant to be a "typical" vision, a Redheaded woodpecker appears to the lamenter and says repeatedly, "Be attentive, and have no fear." Notice the relation of this discipline to the Zen practice of mindfulness, which is likewise an opening of the self to the world. And as the elders interpret the vision of the lamenter upon the latter's return, it is this that they emphasize: "O *Wakan Tanka*, help us always to be attentive!" Or as Thoreau puts it: "No method or discipline can supersede the necessity of being forever on the alert. What is a course of history or philosophy or poetry, no matter how well selected, or the best society, or the most admirable routine of life, compared with the discipline of looking always at what is to be seen" (*Walden*, 411)?

Or consider the Sun Dance. Here, one is *pierced*. Pegs are inserted into the skin and one is then tied by them to a sacred tree. One dances to express one's connection to the tree, and to Mother Earth. In preparing for the dance, Kablaya, the inventor of the dance, was reported by Black Elk to have said this:

"A round circle should be cut and painted red, and this will represent Earth. She is sacred, for upon Her we place our feet, and from her we send our voices to *Wakan Tanka*. She is a relative of ours, and this we should always remember when we call Her 'Grandmother' or 'Mother.' When we pray we raise our hand to the heavens, and afterwards we touch the earth, for is not our spirit from *Wakan Tanka*, and are not our bodies from the earth? We are related to all things: the earth and the stars, everything, and with all these together we raise our hand to *Wakan Tanka* and pray to Him alone." (*The Sacred Pipe*, 72)

The gesture of prayer, which in many cultures consists of a closing off or a movement inward on oneself, is here an opening to and acknowledgment of the powers of the universe.

Indeed, the ceremonial cycle that culminates in the Sun Dance is described by Eagle Man as a cycle of birth. One first purifies oneself in an *Inipi*, or sweat lodge. In this dark, circular space, steam rises from heated stones: The atmosphere is womblike. Eagle Man writes:

> A natural bonding begins within the misty, generative womb of Mother Earth—a bonding to one's own concept of God, the Creator, and the created Mother, upon which we all thrive daily. The spiritual bond is likened to an attachment to Mother Earth as one sits within her warm womb.[4]

One of the points of the *Inipi* ceremony is that, as a mother shares her bodily fluids with the fetus growing within her, the sweat lodge mingles the fluids of the earth and the participants:

> The four directions are called upon within the lodge. The misty, fire-heated steam covers you, bringing forth your own mist (your sweat). Your universal lifeblood comes forth and intermingles with the misty waters of your brothers and sisters around you. The waters of the world (the bucket of water), which have been brought into the lodge, join and mix with the air of the four directions when the dipper of water is ladled onto the hot stones, making steam. The four winds will carry the life blood out of the lodge to the four quarters of our planet. A part of your life blood will seep back into our mother earth. (62)

After being purified in the sweat lodge, one is ceremonially pierced. Pegs are inserted through one's skin, and one is attached by leather thongs to a cottonwood tree. One then dances, pausing every so often to move toward the tree and embrace it, kiss it, or even offer it pieces of one's own flesh. (That procedure is described in *The Sacred Pipe*, but for understandable reasons seems to have been dropped from the much more recent accounts by Eagle Man.) Eagle Man describes the thong as the umbilical that attaches you to your mother the earth. (Women do not dance the Sun Dance, though they participate in other ways, and Eagle Man's explanation is that they do not need to, as they are capable of experiencing the pain of birth by *giving* birth.) Eagle Man's description continues:

> After the fourth touching of the tree, the dancers lean back against the ropes. Now they are free to seek their own Sun Dance vision. All gathered that day are concentrating once again as a nation up to the ultimate and out to the relationship of all that is upon the Mother. This is a profound power of the Sun Dance. After a while, the dancers lean back to break the umbilical with the Mother. Sometimes they have to lean very hard. The peg tears through the skin, and this part is not as painful as most people imagine. Sometimes the pegs will shoot across the arena when they come loose. (95)

The symbolism involved here is beautiful and profound. The Sun Dance is an enactment of human situation, an acknowledgment and explication of embeddedness in the real. Notice, first, that this acknowledgment requires pain, or shock; in that sense, it is an "awakening" and a self-effacement before the real. But second, the attachment to the earth which is the source of pain—indeed, the source of the possibility of pain—is celebrated in a dance of thanksgiving. One gives thanks to the universe *even as the universe is damaging one in virtue of one's attachment to it.*

This is a love for the real in the sense I have been using the term 'love,' an allowance of things to be. Then, as one breaks one's fetters, one celebrates, again in pain (for this, too, is as painful as it is beautiful), that one is, within the world, a distinct thing. These two acknowledgments—of attachment and distinction—constitute an enactment and a description of human situation in the real. And notice that the fundamental or radical arena of this acknowledgment is precisely birth: The male child, according to Freud, undergoes precisely this process as an Oedipal drama; one's attachment to the mother is both comforting and dangerous—comforting in its allowance of absorption into nurturing and dangerous in its threat of engulfment. But all of us, men and women, are in this predicament with regard to the world. If there is a "structure" of "dasein," that is it: the oscillation between allowance of the real and flight from it.

Lakota ceremony as a whole presents a way of turning oneself toward or into the world, a way of expressing reverence for the earth. One gives thanks for being nurtured by the earth, but one also acknowledges, and enacts within the ceremony, the pain of living on the earth that is the earth's own pain. Now these are the ceremonies of a devastated people, a people who know as well as it is possible to know what it means to be brutalized, what a toll living in the world can exact. They could have turned away from the world, and many did. But their ceremonies were a way of holding on to the world, even as they were a way of holding on to their culture. The traditionalist *revival* of Lakota culture was also a refreshment in the real, a way of returning out of brutalization into the light of day.

It is a key to all of these points that the structure of representation in Lakota ceremonial, and in Native American cultures as a whole, is different from that of the West. This follows, indeed, from the characterization of representation given above. One *could not* represent the world as it is represented, say, in the Western pictorial tradition and still fully acknowledge one's situatedness. Recall here Emerson's statement that the world globes itself in a drop of dew, that God appears in his entirety in a piece of moss. It would follow from this, I think, that if one found oneself wanting to represent God, one could do it simply by holding up a piece of moss. In Lakota ceremonial, every item—sage, for example, stone, wood, smoke—is the world in germ and hence is an embodiment of *Wakan Tanka*. These items are capable of representing the real in virtue of themselves being real, and hence standing in a relation of summary or exemplification to the world. They are thus something more than "pictures" of the world.

Lame Deer gives this example of representation:

What do you see here, my friend? Just an ordinary old cooking pot, black with soot and full of dents.

It is standing on the fire on top of that old wood stove, and the water bubbles and moves the lid as the white steam rises to the ceiling. Inside the pot is boiling water, chunks of meat with bone and fat, plenty of potatoes.

It doesn't seem to have a message, that old pot, and I guess you don't give it a thought. Except the soup smells good and reminds you that you are hungry. Maybe you are worried that this is dog stew. Well, don't worry. It's just beef—no fat puppy for a special ceremony. It's just an ordinary, everyday meal.

But I'm an Indian. I think about ordinary, common things like this pot. The bubbling water comes from the rain cloud. It represents the sky. The fire comes from the sun which warms us all—men, animals, trees. The meat stands for the four-legged creatures, our animal brothers, who gave of themselves so that we should live. The steam is living breath. (107)

Each aspect of the pot and its contents "globes" the earth, and is fraught with symbolic significance. Yet *what it means* to be a symbol or representation here is in tension with aspects of the Western tradition.

Nevertheless, notice that symbol as encapsulization is, as a matter of fact, present in the representations of the Western tradition as well—paintings are made out of wood and pigment, after all. In that sense, a painting *is* what it represents; or, to put it more clearly, a painting is of the same "order of reality" as what it depicts, if it depicts something real. But notice that the history of Western intellectual treatments of depiction has depended on a (very obscure) notion of an ontological gap between picture and object. This gap has been traditional at least since Book 10 of the *Republic*. Pictures, on this view, are less than fully real, and thus have the power to seduce us into unreality: On this claim, for example, are based various western iconoclasms. This is associated, too, with an epistemology. I am not sure whether the unreality of pictures is supposed to account for the unreality (or different ontological status) of mental images—that is, for the separation of mind from the order of nature—or whether the separation of mind from the order of nature is supposed to account for the unreality of pictures. Either way, the theory of representation gets elaborated or exemplified in an entire metaphysics.

It is likewise wholly in keeping with the ontological egalitarianism of the Lakota tradition that pieces of the world are used to represent the world. (Again, pieces of the world are also used to represent the world in the Western tradition, but there this activity is entangled with an illusion of ontological distinction.) In the Western tradition, representation places us at a distance from its object. But in the Lakota tradition, as Lame Deer says, representation is used precisely to show the web of the real in which we are entangled. As he fought at Wounded Knee, Black Elk rubbed earth on himself as a prayer and as a way of showing that he knew he was himself made of earth. And he says that every tipi represents the entire universe: The circle has no end and contains all things, and the tipi is circular. The same is often said of the fire circle around which people gather and which symbolizes the sacred hoop of the directions. Home and community, thus, operate as representations of the universe, and this is a way of showing their essential identity as a series of nested circles on a single ontological plane.

When Buffalo Calf Woman brought the pipe to the Oglala, she explained that it both contained the world as a whole and was an altar to it:

> Holding the pipe up with its stem to the heavens, she said: "With this sacred pipe you will walk upon the Earth; for the Earth is your Grandmother and Mother, and She is sacred. Every step that is taken upon her should be a prayer. The bowl of the pipe is of red stone; it is the Earth. Carved in the stone and facing the center is the buffalo calf who represents all the four-leggeds who live upon your Mother. The stem of the pipe is of wood, and this represents all that grows upon the Earth. And these twelve feathers which hang here where the stem fits into the bowl are from *Wanbli Galeshka*, the Spotted Eagle, and they represent the eagle and all the wingeds of the air. All these peoples, and all the things of the universe, are joined to you who smoke the pipe—all send their voices to *Wakan Tanka*, the Great Spirit. When you pray with this pipe, you pray for and with everything." (*The Sacred Pipe*, 6)

I think that is one of the most beautiful and profound passages in world literatures. The pipe is the world in germ, not by *depicting* the world in a Western sense but by "globing" it, to use Emerson's word.

When the pipe is loaded, tobacco or willow bark is placed in the pipe for each of the four directions, for the earth and *Wakan Tanka*, for the various families of animals, and so on, so that the pipe comes to contain the world. Then the tobacco or bark is lighted, and one takes the world into one's own body. One becomes the world, in an experience characteristic of mystical experiences in many cultures. But then, as is true also of the Sun Dance, there is a moment of *releasing* the world back out of oneself and into . . . the world itself. For this reason, smoke is the perfect medium of the ceremony, for it disperses slowly and imperceptibly into the entire atmosphere. Again, this is a deep enactment of situation, or simultaneous merging of the self into the other and releasing of the other from the self that leads to one's own distinction within things. One takes the smoke, which is the world, into the open place within one, and then *releases* it.

It is hardly surprising, therefore, that the pipe ceremony is associated with truth. Eagle Man says that "The smoke from the pipe represents the participants' visible breath and stands for truth: truthful words, truthful actions, and a truthful spirit" (57). To find the truth, here, means to find in oneself a space sufficient for the entire world and to find in oneself also the capacity to allow the world to return into externality, accompanied by a prayer and a giving of thanks. The Sioux holy man Fools Crow sings the following prayer for self-knowledge:

> Great Ones
> Pity Me
> Help me look honestly at myself.
> Truth is coming.
> It hurts me.
> I am glad.[5]

All views about representation are also views about power. In the west, again, we exercise our power by "generalizing" and "distancing" and "abstracting," all of which are movements away from concrete situation. That is, we remove the particular lives of things from those things in order to gain control of them. We make the powerless pay with their lives, as we pay for the exercise of our power over our selves with our own lives. We control things by depicting or textualizing them; we shunt them away and hold them for use. The power of the pipe is, on the contrary, an ever deeper commitment to things, an act of love toward things in their full-blooded existence as threats or delights to, releasers or destroyers of, the self. One is powerful here because one holds in one's hand or in one's lungs the world in germ, because one has and one is a microcosm of all that is. "Nothing can live well except in a manner that is suited to the way the sacred Power of the World lives and moves" (*Black Elk Speaks*, 208). One is powerful as an expression of the world's power; one hooks up with the world's power by acts of veneration for the world. One can, thus, "make things happen," not in the sense of forcing things to happen but in the sense of allowing things to happen in the world one is. Fools Crow says that he and Black Elk agreed that, as healers, they themselves exercised no power but that they were "holes" or "hollow bones" through which the powers of the world acted (*Fools Crow*, 50). As in Taoism, power here is an emptying of the self into the world rather than an intensification of self. In this sense, power is openness to things; power is truth.

Power, in this sense, has its origin in love, in the free space of truth of which Heidegger wrote. Lame Deer heard a voice that said to him:

"You have love for all that has been placed on this earth, not like the love of a mother for her son, or of a son for his mother, but a bigger love which encompasses the whole earth. You are just a human being, afraid, weeping under that blanket, but there is a great space within you to be filled with that love. All of nature can fit in there." (139)

And Black Elk says: "The good road and the road of difficulties you have made to cross; and where they cross, the place is holy. Day in and day out forever, you are the life of things" (*Black Elk Speaks*, 272).

6

SEDUCTION, TRANSGRESSION, ADDICTION

Every philosophy expresses the experience of the philosopher. There is no truth so obvious, no argument so compelling, that it cannot be staved off indefinitely by a professional. I believe, finally, what I need to believe, and write, finally, what I need to write: either what I need to *hear* so badly that I reach for the desperate expedient of saying it to myself on the printed page or what I am constrained to defend because of what I am. The arguments I then enunciate, if any, give the positions thus arrived at the patina of objective respectability, but the oomph of the position has nothing to do with arguments. When Quine says that he has a taste for desert landscapes, for example, he is much closer to the heart of his ontology than when he actually argues about what there is.

I.

I have been taught about reality by a hard teacher, a teacher that left me nowhere to squirm, so that I had to sit and listen: alcoholism and drug addiction. I started smoking marijuana when I was fourteen, and I smoked every day (and, most days, several times a day) for fifteen years. I drank alcoholically—that is, without being able to control my drinking once I had started—for at least ten years. I had various encounters with cocaine (including crack), LSD, and a variety of other drugs. My father died at age 49 from the combined effect of addictions (though he was sober when he died, of emphysema). One of my brothers was killed in a PCP-related murder; another brother died of a heroin overdose; yet another did five years in the state pen for a heroin-driven armed robbery. I have lost jobs, flipped cars, and so forth.

I say this not to arouse your pity (though what the heck, pity if you like; better yet, send cash) but to emphasize the extent of the craziness and the extent of my motivation to stop what I was doing. Any fool could see that I ought to stop using drugs and alcohol, and only an idiot would continue. Indeed, what stunned me continually, besides the substances, was the weakness of my will. From the teenager who viewed himself as the Nietzschean overman, ready to give the world a dose of Will to Power, I had become a person who could not stop himself from pouring vodka down his own throat. By the end, when I was drinking secretly all day, every day, I hated myself for drinking and drugging; but I hated myself more for what those acts showed about my *strength*: namely, that I didn't have any. I wanted to stop. Indeed, I wanted nothing else so much as to stop. And I could continue to want to stop even as I was raising the bottle to my lips. My body seemed to be operating independently of my will.

Now this experience, the experience of being out of control, of having one's will broken, is, I assert, in germ, the most profound and also the most typical experience of which human beings are capable. It is the experience of *coming up against what is real*. Even the most powerful will in the world, and even if that will is attached to the most powerful intellect and the most powerful body, has a *tiny* field of action, supposing for a moment that the notion that it has any field of action at all is not an illusion. My ability to shift a weight, to move from one place to another, to acquire things or to dispose of them, could increase a thousandfold and still be minuscule in proportion to the world in general. And my exercise of such capacities as I do have to lift, to travel, to acquire, or whatever is both fixed by and articulated within the way things are. To travel by plane I must get to the airport, take the scheduled flight, and so on and so forth. If it is by the free exercise of will that I travel, I do so under ubiquitous constraint.

Everywhere my will turns, it runs up against reality like a brick wall. In fact, so powerful are these constraints that I literally cannot will what I know reality does not allow me the hope of accomplishing: I can no more *try* to jump over the moon than I *can* jump over the moon. This fact allows my will to be approximately proportioned to my capacities, so that the limitations of the latter do not rise constantly to consciousness. I cannot jump over the moon, or even over my desk, so I can forget that I cannot, and take pleasure in the fact that I can hop a foot into the air and shoot a basketball. There is nothing wrong with the pleasure. But such pleasures are bought at the cost of forgetfulness; every pleasure we take at the exercise of our capacities is the avoidance of a million pains at our incapacities. Every little capacity we have is a tiny zone carved out of a crushing universe. It is this that allows us to feel "free." The freedom we enjoy is the product of a massive forgetting, and what is forgotten is the real. To feel free is to forget the world.

We live our lives in a continual pattern of pushing against the world and having the world push back against us. The manner and direction of our pushing is our situation. Among other things, this dynamic is the source of great pleasure. For example, this structure is displayed with crystalline purity in the act of weight lifting. I go to the gym and lift weights for several purposes: to look good, improve my health, and so forth. But fundamentally, I go there not to accomplish any particular purpose but simply to push at the weights and to be pushed at by the weights. And I suspect that other people respond as I do, or they could not keep coming back again and again. I need, first of all, to feel myself as a person who is capable of making things happen, but I need, even more, I think, to feel myself to be a person who is *in*capable of making things happen. I work each set to failure; that is, I am finished only when I can no longer move the weight. To feel oneself lifting a weight is to feel the world resisting one's will. To seek the experience of lifting weights until one can no longer move the weight is to seek the experience of this resistance and to take pleasure in reality, that is, in one's incapacity. What is experienced at the edge of one's capacity is, despite the artificiality of the environment, experienced as real because of its resistance to will. And to experience the real consciously is to have an authentic experience, which, as Emerson and Thoreau assert, is what we crave.

Now, as I say, we devote most of our technological effort, for example, not to "improving the quality of life" per se, but to ameliorating our sense of situation, to desituating ourselves. We yearn for this as an escape from danger and animality, but we yearn also, and perhaps more deeply, for situation. Indeed, this book is an expression of the latter yearning. And so is weight lifting, which is motivated by the desire to embed oneself totally in situation, to explore the limits of will and the limits of bodily action in response to will. A gym is a device for testing these capacities with absolute specificity and systematicity: One moves from exercise to exercise, testing one or another muscle or driving each muscle to failure. Now exercise is addictive. And what addicts is not the exercise of will as one pushes out against the weight but the failure of will as the weight pushes back. It is *resistance* and, finally, *failure in the face of resistance* that flood the brain with endorphins. That is, it is not the exercise of power that addicts but the response of the world to the exercise of power, the demonstration of one's powerlessness. The encounter with the real is the encounter with one's own failure, and failure always "brings home the reality" of situation.

Pushing the weight away from one's body in, say, the bench press is the attempt to push the world away from oneself, to shift the burden of the real by an act of personal power. The grunt of weight lifter, his concentration and aggressiveness, are expressions of personal power and measurements of it. But one goes to the gym knowing that one will fail or, indeed, intending to fail, in the sense that one will end up trying to lift the weight one more time than one can actually lift it or trying to lift five more pounds than one can lift. And thus, it is not the power of strength that addicts one to lifting; it is the powerlessness of failure. One presses against the world, but only for the purpose of feeling the world press back even harder. Indeed, this dynamic informs and infests every human perversity and addiction.

For example, as I think I've said, I enjoy thunderstorms. Every time I see one coming up, I hope that it is extremely intense. This, I think, is in part because of the illusion of safety, and the reality of protection from the weather, created by a climate-controlled house. The intensity of a storm, its loudness and so forth, teach me or suggest to me that I am vulnerable to the world: are, for me, a ritual enactment of the limits of my will. Here we see precisely the same dynamic as with weight lifting, but now on a cultural or collective scale: The building of homes such as I live in is a pushing out of the world, a lifting of the weight of reality. The storm is reality pressing back. Thus, too, we all enjoy natural disasters, when they are depicted on television. Here, without actually being, say, crushed by the earthquake or burned alive by the fire, I get a sense of the limitations of my will; I feel the limits of human power. Thus, in all these cases, I get the pleasure of "letting go," the pleasure of "the burn" or utter exhaustion, when my will no longer operates. That will can be experienced as a burden is one of the dominant themes played out in human history.

Sex, too, plays in the same space. The mating ritual is an elaborate drama of power between the sexes. A man (let us say) tries to bend a woman to his will, tests the limits of his power in the arena of her body. He wants her resistance—indeed, is perhaps incapable of sexual desire where there is no resistance; at any rate, each resistance intensifies desire, and each sort of resistance calls forth a certain sort of desire. Thus, sex can become an incredibly elaborate ritualized enactment of resistances and the overcoming of resistances: All the impedimenta of bondage and discipline are designed to bring this dynamic to a fever pitch. But sex culminates in a loss of self, a letting go of will, which men enact in the most literal physical sense: Orgasm makes men limp; the culmination of passion is precisely loss of power and loss of desire.

The dynamic that finds expression in all these ways takes on a peculiar form in the case of substance abuse. Notice that abused substances, like barbells, are pieces of the external world. And notice that the addict moves these substances around until he is incapable of moving anything; I always drank toward oblivion, toward the final loss of will, toward death. Alcohol, cocaine, and the like are *toxic*, poisonous. "Substance abuse" is a particularly thorough expression of the dynamic of resistance, for it issues not in the temporary oblivion and loss of will of orgasm but in an oblivion and loss of will that permeate one's life. In addiction, the zone of the exercise of my will narrowed to almost nothing, or perhaps really to nothing. For here it was *my own body* that I could not control. The same lesson can be learned from physical handicaps, grinding sickness, and so forth. To experience myself as an addict was to experience myself as real: to experience myself as recalcitrant to the activity of my own will. Here, the weight I am pushing is myself, the ritual enactment of resistance takes place *internally*, precisely in one's own relation to one's will.

For that is one mark of the real: its recalcitrance to human will. It is a fact that if I stroll in front of a Mack truck which is traveling at sixty miles an hour, I will pop. That is a pretty good demonstration that Mack trucks are real. If I could will the thing away at the last second, I could not even entertain myself with that activity, because the truck would be, and I would know it to be, a figment of my imagination. Now, of course, there are some things that may be recalcitrant to my will that do not straightforwardly exist. For example, I cannot will Hamlet forward into action before the last act. So (though I could go on from this into an ontology, and though I won't) we might say that recalcitrance to will is a necessary though not sufficient condition for reality. More, it is a typical *mark* of the real, a sign that something is going on. Thus, every experience of powerlessness, every awareness of limits imposed upon one, is experienced as the impingement of the real.

Compulsion is powerlessness over one's own body; obsession is powerlessness over one's own mind. (They are, finally, the same thing.) When the recalcitrance and poignancy that one usually experiences in relation to the external world comes to be experienced in relation to oneself, then one has become, to oneself, part of the world; one has become real to oneself. To experience oneself as powerless over oneself is to experience oneself as fully real: it is to experience oneself in exactly the same way that one experiences "external" objects. It is no accident that every mystical discipline that has as its goal the identification of the self with the other, of subject and object, person and world, starts with a letting go of will. To let go of one's will is to experience oneself as one with things. And though I have tried to let go of will in this mystical fashion, I have found that the fact that one lets go of will by an act of will is an embarrassment to the experience one is cultivating. It is better, as far as this is concerned, to have one's will *humbled*: to have it demonstrated to one that one is part of the external world in an experience of oneself as being out of one's own control.

Thus, the experience of addiction leads to what seems to be an odd sort of confusion between the inner and the outer, a confusion in which the self is external to itself, in which the self is other. In addiction, the distinction between what is internal and what is external to oneself breaks down. For example, addiction often carries with it the burden of certain sorts of secrecies. I drank secretly for years. I am not sure who knew what about my drinking, but I expended prodigious efforts to keep anyone from knowing anything. This was an attempt, in a certain way, to keep myself outside the real by refusing to allow myself to leak into the real. That is, my drinking was somehow not fully actual if *I* was the only one who knew about it. Thus, I had a stake in an absolute distinction of myself from situation, a stake which motivated me to drink more, since the experience of disorientation is at once a letting go into willessness and a flight from reality. It was seeing this distinction *break down* precisely at the moment of its greatest distance that taught me how to stop drinking. That is, at the end of a drunk, and also at the end of drunks, just before death or recovery, the distinction between the inner and the outer breaks down. Telling lies becomes lying to oneself; passing out is merging into the world. Thus, to practice secrecy is to learn publicity. The self at its greatest intensity becomes external to itself and is experienced as a thing among other things.

Zen and Taoist monks have, for centuries, used drunkenness as a propaedeutic to mystical experience as well as a recreation. For notice that the state of inebriation is precisely the humbling of the will: a "letting go." I experience my will as the barrier between myself and myself; I yearn to *allow* myself to do what I would do if I were incapable of controlling myself. And to achieve *that*, substance abuse is the best means known to man. I want, for example, to break through the constraints of society, perhaps at a party. But the intolerable thing about the "constraints of society" is that, unless I am in prison or something, I *experience* them not as constraints placed on me by society but as constraints placed on me by the operation of my own will. Why can't I dance like a madman or scream at the top of my lungs or piss on the cat? Not because *you'll stop me*, but because *I can't allow myself to*. Georges Bataille puts the point like this:

> The truth of taboos is the truth of our human attitude. We must know, we can know that prohibitions are not imposed from without. This is clear to us in the anguish we feel when we are violating the taboo, especially at the moment when our feelings hang in the balance, when the taboo still holds good and yet we are yielding to the impulsion it forbids. If we observe the taboo, if we submit to it, we are no longer conscious of it. But in the act of violating it we feel the anguish of mind without which the taboo could not exist: that is the experience of sin. That experience leads to the completed transgression, the successful transgression which, in maintaining the prohibition, maintains it in order to benefit by it. The inner experience of eroticism demands from the subject a sensitiveness to the anguish at the heart of the taboo no less than the desire which leads him to infringe it. This is religious sensibility, and it always links desire closely with terror, intense pleasure and anguish.[1]

Transgression does not free the transgressor of the taboo. On the contrary, to transgress is to acknowledge the power of the taboo, a power that is in the transgressor if it is power at all. The consciousness of this power, and the simultaneous necessity of its transgression, is, for Bataille, anguish and the religious sensibility. One can only overcome the values that have a life within oneself, and in this overcoming, the value is reinscribed.

Yet the causation of taboo and transgression is mutual and simultaneous. The taboo is incomprehensible without the sensibility of transgression. We need no values to protect us from things that we do not feel possible for ourselves as transgressions. Thus, the taboo inscribes the transgression also. What is seductive for us gathers taboos around it, and what is taboo gains, in being prohibited, a seductive power. Thus, to transgress simultaneously draws us into the social space of values and releases us into the space beyond or before sociality.

To get drunk is to experience the relaxation of the faculty of self-control or internalized taboo, which is also the state sought through meditation. Finally, what one seeks through intoxication (and, on Bataille's account, eroticism and the religious) is oblivion, or death: One seeks to become literally an inanimate object, that is, to become a thing among things. The only possible irony of this activity is that one is already a thing among things, that the will that is experienced as importunate and powerful is, in fact, pathetically limited. But, as I say, we experience the exercise of power within the tiny limits of our capacity much more vividly than we experience the huge extent of what we cannot effect by any act of will.

Vice, then, forces us into the real precisely by *seducing us into oblivion.* Every seduction, in fact, is an invitation to oblivion and an appeal to the need of the seduced for self-forgetting. Socrates famously argued that no man desires what is evil, that evil is always the result of ignorance. That is true to this extent: Falling into evil is always a letting go of oneself, always a seduction. Bataille writes:

> What I have been saying refers to this void and nothing else.
>
> But the void opens at a specific point. Death, for instance, may open it: the corpse into which death infuses absence, the putrefaction associated with this absence. I can link my revulsion at the decay (my imagination suggests it, not my memory, so profoundly is it a forbidden object for me) with the feelings that obscenity arouses in me. I can tell myself that repugnance and horror are the mainsprings of my

desire, that such desire is only aroused as long as its object causes a chasm no less deep than death to yawn within me, and that this desire originates in its opposite, horror. (*Erotism*, 59)

Desire, in this sense, is a chasm, something into which we tumble, and our desire for desire springs from a need to tumble into this chasm.

To fall into evil is to let go into and finally to let go even of desire, to be "swept away." And to tumble into evil is always experienced, hence, as a loss of freedom, or, at any rate, as a loss of will; of course, that is precisely what we need. But Socrates' view is false for this reason: that we all, more or less openly, desire to be seduced by vice, to let ourselves go. There is nothing, no horror in the horrible history of humanity, of which each of us is not capable, if only we could be seduced in the right way. Montaigne once remarked with true profundity that there was no crime that he could not imagine himself committing. To be able to say that is to have experienced vice, though not necessarily to have met vice without resistance.

Evil, since the Garden, has always appeared as a seduction. And we have need of it, now as always: It is the only cure for the surfeit of will from which we seem to ourselves to suffer. To allow oneself to do evil can be to relax into the nature of things, not because the nature of things is evil but because evil can constitute an allowance to be. We have constrained ourselves, or we experience ourselves as the constrainers of ourselves and of one another. Thus we must *transgress*, and we must *allow ourselves to be transgressed*. As I have argued, or rather asserted, values can be constructed in a negation of reality; these values tell us that what exists is inadequate, by telling us what ought to be. Thus self-conscious transgression of one's own values can be an affirmation of what is. In this sense, transgression is a sacrament; to transgress one's own values is to say *yes*: the particular *yes* that is a letting go into seduction, an allowing of oneself to be seduced. As Bataille saw, seduction connects transgression and death as a oneness with bodies: "Eroticism . . . is assenting to life up to the point of death" (*Erotism*, 11). This is why we need our vices, need our crimes, need more or less every horror that has ever been perpetrated. And, by the way, we also need our horror in response to transgression; we need something to transgress.

The odd thing about the structure of addiction is that when one comes no longer to experience the use of, say, alcohol as a transgression of values, one loses one's compulsion to drink. That is, when I found that I *could* not stop drinking, I could stop drinking. The addiction, for me, was a cycle of attempted impositions of will followed by the inevitable seduction into vice. But as soon as I acknowledged that I simply had no will in the matter, as soon as I acknowledged, hence, that drinking could not be a seduction or a transgression, I no longer had to drink. This was fortunate for me, I think, because, though oblivion and death are seductive—or rather, are the seductive per se—I found myself, and find myself, with an impulse to remain alive. And I would not have long remained alive as I was going. Thus, I had to proceed to other transgressions, petty though they may be—transgressions such as writing philosophy that cannot be published in philosophy journals.

II.

Bataille connects transgression to the religious sensibility, and many of these notions are thematized in Tantrism, an Indian movement that has taken place both within Buddhism and Hinduism (as well as outside of both in local cults in India and Nepal) and that is associated with the worship of Kali, the dark goddess of creative destruction and consort of Siva, a god given to Dionysian violations.

I think it is fair to say that all the cults and movements which derive from the incredibly powerful source of the Vedas and the Upanishads (Tantrism does so derive, though it also possesses elements of the aboriginal goddess worship of the subcontinent) are characterized by ecstatic monism. The fundamental thought of all Vedic teachings is that *there is only one thing*: Brahman, which could be understood as a god, or as the Absolute: the one thing that truly is. This monism immediately raises the question of the ontological status of the things we encounter in this world. For what we seem to encounter in this world is a plurality of things, a many, a "blooming, buzzing confusion." And as that phrase of William James indicates, this world of things is in constant change, change that would be beneath the dignity of, and conceptually incompatible with, Brahman as the Absolute. In the similar cosmology of the Eleatics, for example, it was proven that motion was impossible.

Thus, despite the world-affirming tone of the early Upanishads, the orthodox development of Hindu philosophy through Shankara's Vedanta was the history of a careful distinction between Brahman and *maya*, the veil of appearance, or *samsara*, the cycle of becoming. *Maya*'s primordial sense is "illusion," or, better, "magic trick." If there is only one thing, but appear to be many things, then what causes this appearance must be a feat of legerdemain. Then Vedantic spiritual discipline would consist in a penetration of *maya* to Brahman: a withdrawal from and renunciation of the apparent world for immersion in the One Thing That Is. Such an immersion would be, simultaneously, an escape from *samsara*, an escape from becoming and into being, often expressed or symbolized as an escape from the cycle of reincarnation.

Now I would not presume to refute thousands of years of philosophy in a paragraph, or rather I would, but not before saying I would not. But it is worth pointing out that this distinction between Brahman and *maya* is a mess. If there is only one thing, and that thing is the unchanging Absolute, then the fact that we are embedded in a world of flying appearances is incomprehensible. Whence these appearances, and whereto? And whence and whereto myself as the experiencer of these appearances? Just as Vedanta had to distinguish carefully between Brahman and *maya*, it had to distinguish carefully between the apparent self, the self as separate from what is (from the rest of *maya* as well as from Brahman), and the true self: *Atman.* The Chandogya Upanishad says, first of all, that "this whole world is Brahman," and famously adds, "*Tat tvam asi*" (that art thou). *You are* Brahman, and hence *you are* the world.

Now, this motivated philosophers to say that *maya* is unreal and that the self that lives in *maya* is unreal. Inside, underneath, or transcending the apparent world and the apparent self that experiences it is the real world and the real self that experiences *that.* Thus, Hinduism developed into a world-negating doctrine and a guide to *escape* (*moksa*, or the *nirvana* of Buddhism). But, of course, these passages (and hundreds more in the same spirit) admit of a very different reading. They are most naturally read as suggesting that *nothing could be more real* than this world, that this world is perfectly real, absolutely real, that *this* world is Brahman. In other words, the basic Upanishadic doctrine of monism could be used to motivate a meticulous distinction of appearance from reality, or it could be used to motivate an absolute identification of the two. And note that the drawing of distinctions of this type is, in fact, incompatible with the monism that motivated the distinctions in the first place. That is, the claim that there is only one thing does not comport very well with meticulously sorting things into categories. The presence *even of illusions* such as *maya* and *samsara* and the phenomenal self is incompatible with Vedic monism.

Tantrism (at least in certain of its aspects and expressions) can be understood as a return to the primordial monism of the Upanishads. For Tantra asserts the reality of the world around us, and renounces any mode of escape or evasion. In the history of world religions, only Taoism approaches the Tantric cults in affirmation of the world. Though *maya* can be rendered as "trick or illusion," it is also the *magic* of Brahman, the way Brahman is manifest, Brahman's power or female aspect, or *shakti*. That is why Tantrism has taken the form of goddess worship: To worship the goddess is to worship Brahman *in* and *as* the universe, renouncing all escape, denial, evasion. It is a worship of *shakti*, the power and mystery of this real world. There is no way out of the universe; we can only go more and more deeply in.

In traditional Vedic ethics, there are four ends of human life: *artha* (material wealth), *kama* (sensual gratification), *dharma* (obedience to law and moral duty), and *moksa* (release or liberation). Vedantic thought tended to range these ends in a hierarchy and relate them to social classes, so that the highest persons pursue what is the ultimate goal of human life: *moksa*. The brahmin is supposed to renounce the other purposes in the pursuit of *moksa*, which is, precisely, a liberation from these other aspects of human life. On the other hand, it is not surprising, given the world-affirming basis of Tantrism, that Tantrism also affirms all the human desires. Just as the Absolute *is* the contingent, liberation *is* wealth, *is* sex, *is* right action. One does not achieve liberation by transcending the normal range of human desires (that is, by ascetic discipline) but by immersion in one's humanity. One finds enlightenment precisely where one already is, in what one already does. The only *nirvana* we seek is the *nirvana* we already have. As Heinrich Zimmer puts it: "The ideal of Tantrism is to achieve illumination precisely by means of those very objects which the earlier sages sought to banish from their consciousness."[2] We do not seek to find the Brahman behind the *maya*, the *samsara*, the apparent self, but precisely within them; for we are always within them.

The illusion, for Tantrism, is not *maya*; *maya* is *shakti*, reality manifest, the power of the real. The illusion, rather, is ego, or what I have been calling will, the experience of separation from the world, that operates in persons as the feeling that we can or should exercise *power* over the world. But even this illusion, finally, is to be experienced, is to be savored; it can be penetrated only by moving toward it as powerfully as possible—sexually, for instance. For Tantrism, too, though it is a logical extension of monism, is also capable of acknowledging plurality: of acknowledging the self and the other. If one lost one's ego or will in a total identification with the universe, one would not be in a position to enjoy the gratifications that life offers. As Ramakrishna, the great Tantric master of the nineteenth century, put it: "The devotee of God wants to eat sugar, not become sugar."[3] Here, plurality and unity are seen to be interdependent; if we are to affirm the reality of *maya*, we must affirm of the one thing that is that it is manifest in each of the many things that are.

This point is emphasized in a discussion of Tibetan Buddhist Tantra by Chogyam Trungpa, Rinpoche:

> We are concerned with what actual reality is. Is reality a gap, a crack, or is reality a big sheet of cloth, all-pervasive? In the non-theistic tradition of Buddhist tantra, when we begin to have a relationship with the world, we do not try to make sure the world is part of us. In fact, the question of separation does not come up at all. According to the non-theistic tradition, we do not believe ourselves to be creatures. We are some kind of being—or nonbeing, for that matter—but we were never created, and therefore we are not particularly creatures. Nevertheless, there is a sense of continuity, without hysteria, without panic, without any congratulatory remarks or attempts to smooth things out. The world exists and we exist. We and the world

are separate from that point of view—but so what? We could regard the separateness as part of the continuity rather than trying to deny it.[4]

As I said in the first chapter, "realism" in the sense used here is not, or anyhow is not meant to be, a philosophical system or structure of assertions: It is a bodily posture of openness to things. I think that attitude is perfectly expressed here by Trungpa. In some sense, the question of unity and plurality is abstract; the *lived experience* of real things in a real world is more important. Any *principle* compromises the affirmation, because it calls us into a loyalty to our interpretation of the world rather than to the world. This overcoming of principles could be expressed as a contradiction: Our distinctness from the world is our identity with it. And that is just to say that we are situated, are embedded; our separateness from the world, our eating of sugar, *is* our identity with the world, our existence among things like sugar. The sugar is enjoyed precisely as it becomes identical with us or gets incorporated within us, but we enjoy the world only as *it* ingests *us*. To be ingested, we must be distinct.

As Trungpa also says:

The maha ati practitioner [one who is on the final stage of the Tantric path] sees a completely naked world, at the level of marrow, rather than skin or flesh or even bones. In the lower yanas [vehicles], we develop lots of idioms and terms, and that makes us feel better because we have lots of things to talk about, such as compassion or emptiness or wisdom. But in fact, that becomes a way of avoiding the actual naked reality of life.[5]

The deep affirmation of the real in Tantrism takes a most profound ritual form, a form relevant to our present concern. For Tantric ritual is a formalized transgression.

Tantric ritual consists of doing what is forbidden. As I have said, the seduction into evil or vice may be, finally, a letting go into things, an affirmation of what is. And Tantrism, in pursuit of religious experience precisely as such affirmation, practices such seduction systematically. The five "forbidden things" of Vedic ethics become precisely the sacraments of Tantrism: wine, meat, fish, parched grain, and sexual intercourse. The *Kama Sutra*, for example, is not, or is not only, a sex manual but a guide to sex as sacrament, and hence a guide to being seduced by reality. Since reality is *shakti*, Tantric sex involves identifying a woman as *shakti*, and then experiencing her completely, in every way possible. What is female, hence, is what is real, and, for a man, losing oneself in sex becomes losing oneself in the real; embedding oneself in a woman is embedding oneself in the real; loving a woman is loving the real; spilling seed in a woman is participating in the mystery of creation that she embodies. The erotic art and literature of India is vast and profound: Sex, including transgressive sex—group sex, homosexual sex, sex with eunuchs, and so forth—becomes sacramental. This is not to say that it is no longer savored as pleasurable; indeed, the sacrament consists in a deeper and deeper pleasure in the body.

Tantrism prescribes a systematic violation of all that the culture within which it is embedded holds most dear: a destruction or suspension of values in an affirmation of desire and the body. The *Guhyasama Tantra* provides one of the most extreme examples, simply by inverting or negating the strictest tenets of Buddhism: "Kill all living beings, let your words be lies, take what is not given, and enjoy the ladies."[6] After quoting that passage, Indra Sinha goes on to summarize the passages that follow: The text "suggests that the sadhaka should take a radiantly lovely sixteen-year old girl, scent her with perfumes and deck her with ornaments, and then have intercourse with her, worshipping her [as an embodiment of *shakti*] with, and offering to the gods, the four essences of his body: excrement, urine, semen, and blood: if he does this, he will become the equal of a buddha." With absolute systematicity, then, Tantrism becomes a celebration of the obscene and despised, and what is above all obscene and despised is whatever reminds us of the body. Using bodily fluids as holy water is an affirmation of embodiment, and that affirmation is what most truly transgresses Buddhism. The great scholar of Tantrism Sir John Woodroffe (Arthur Avalon) wrote that "he who realizes the truth of the body can then come to know the truth of the universe."[7]

It will hardly be surprising, therefore, that the various Tantric movements incorporate intoxication into their rituals. These rituals are always seductions into vice; one feels oneself spinning out of one's own control and into an ecstatic identification with the world. The *Kulanarva-tantra* says that "the adept should drink, drink, and drink again until he falls to the ground. If he gets up and drinks again, he will be freed from rebirth. His happiness enchants the goddess, Lord Bhairava delights in his swooning, his vomiting pleases the gods."[8] To be freed from the wheel of reincarnation is, precisely, to be freed of consciousness, freed from the faculty of judgment.

The *Guhyasama Tantra* also says this: "Perfection can be attained easily by satisfying all desires."[9] It goes without saying that this is a flat contradiction of every sort of asceticism. And, of course, asceticism dominates orthodox Hinduism, Buddhism, and Jainism. But notice that, as ethics is a systematic rejection of reality, asceticism is a systematic rejection of oneself as real. That is, one seeks to purge or mortify or, really, to kill oneself, and one starts with one's desires, particularly, or perhaps only, such desires as remind one that one is an animal and a body. The Tantric sacraments are designed to show that enlightenment is found in the satisfaction of desire, that is, in total commitment to embodiment and the systematic violation of principles. Tantric sexual practices, for example, are designed to bring desire to fever pitch, to intensify desire to the greatest possible extent. For example, the adept may be told to leave his cock in his *shakti*'s cunt for hours without coming.

To repeat, every claim about what ought to be the case is an expression of hatred and fear toward what is the case. Thus, every ethical prohibition is a negation of this world, a flight from *maya*. That is fine—indeed, is necessary—if this world is an illusion, a despicable barrier between us and what really is. But if *maya is* Brahman, if we live right now inside the highest reality there is, then it is ethics, not transgressions of ethics, that are the deepest danger. If *maya* is Brahman, then enlightenment consists of seduction into transgression: Wine and sex are not to be feared, banned, loathed but engaged in as a worship of that which is most high, that is, of Kali, the destroyer, that is, of this world. (Kali appears in art wearing a girdle of human heads.) To make a sacrament of transgression is as deep as religion has ever gone into what it is to be human.

The sanctity of transgression, and hence the sanctity of the world, is a theme of many religions. There are, in India, several transgressive cults, both within and outside of popular Hinduism. The epic of India, the *Mahabharata*, is, to a large extent, the epic of ritual transgression. The Pandavas, the brothers who are the heroes of the epic, are, in some sense, incarnated virtues. Yudishtira, their leader, for example, is supposed to be incapable of speaking an untruth. Arjuna, the war chieftain, scrupulously observes the chivalrous code of warfare. But in the climactic battle with the evil Kauravas, Krishna, who is an incarnation of the Supreme Lord, and thus the author of the ethics which the Pandavas symbolize, urges each of the Pandavas to violate his most sacred principles in order to win the war. Yudishtira, for example, lies to his former teacher Drona, telling him that his (Drona's) son has been killed. Drona, who drops his arms, is then himself killed in his moment of vulnerability. Arjuna is urged by Krishna to kill Karna (who is Arjuna's brother), when Karna's chariot becomes stuck in mud, a clear violation of the rules of warfare. Thus, the plot finally resolves into a long transgression of ethics by the Supreme Lord himself, for the purpose of gaining the world.

The power of transgression is also thematized in Native American religions. Lame Deer, for example, says that he needed precisely transgression to become holy:

> Sickness, jail, poverty, getting drunk—I had to experience all that myself. Sinning makes the world go round. You can't be so stuck up, so inhuman that you want to be pure, your soul wrapped up in a plastic bag, all the time. You have to be God and the devil, both of them. Being a good medicine man means being right in the midst of the turmoil, not shielding yourself from it. It means experiencing life in all its phases. It means not being afraid of cutting up and playing the fool now and then. That's sacred too.
>
> Nature, the Great Spirit—they are not perfect. The world couldn't stand that perfection. The spirit has a good side and a bad side. Sometimes the bad side gives me more knowledge than the good side. (*Lame Deer Seeker of Visions*, 76)

Here, first of all, transgression is not enclosed into the context of ceremony. Lame Deer describes in detail, for instance, an interstate crime spree. That was, among other things, a way of finding out about life and about the world. It was an affirmation of the world in its imperfection, as is Lame Deer's spiritual practice in its entirety.

Barbara Tedlock describes the function of the *heyoka*, or contrary, in Sioux ceremonial as follows:

> During a *heyoka* impersonation, the new *heyoka* does many foolish things, such as riding backwards so that he's coming when he's really going; if the weather is hot he covers himself with blankets and shivers as if

with cold, and he always says 'yes' when he means 'no.' These actions, while they expose him to the ridicule of the unthinking, have important meaning. As Lame Deer expressed it: "fooling around, a clown is really performing a spiritual ceremony."[10]

As Tedlock goes on to argue, the function of the sacred clown in Native American ceremony is to make people laugh, which "opens them to immediate experience." Tedlock describes an Eskimo custom to the effect that a ceremony cannot begin until everyone has laughed—that is, until everyone has been opened by comedic transgression into situation. Pueblo clowns, writes Tedlock, often wore enormous dildoes during ceremonies, and among the Maidu of California, a clown accompanies the shaman during the most holy ceremonies, parodying and ridiculing him as the ceremony is performed.

We Westerners, too, have our ritualized transgressions, our clowns, and so forth. Rock stars, comedians, and, for that matter, artists are allowed to ridicule our leaders and institutions and to engage in public displays of debauchery. This performs a *religious* function for us in that it keeps our lives and our worship, always threatening to come unmoored from the world in imagination, open to what is. To laugh is precisely to open oneself, and humor is often, or perhaps always, transgressive. That is why humorlessness is always suspicious: Solemnity is, in this sense, blasphemy. To take the world seriously always shows that one *invests the world with meaning*—that is, that one flees its contingency and bizarreness into the world of principles and concepts. For that reason, genuine profundity is always found in the company of playfulness. To be playful is to *let go*; it is to seduce and to be seduced, though perhaps in a small way. Finally, solemnity is the virtue from which we may someday perish, while playfulness is the vice that may yet redeem us.

Kali destroys, but more importantly, and connectedly, Kali plays. The treatment of transgression as sacrament

is not supposed to solemnify sex or drinking; it is supposed to add joy to sacrament. Kali enjoys seducing us,
and we, in turn, enjoy being seduced; the *Kama Sutra* is a
guide to pleasure. The opening into and affirmation of what
is real is, finally, a joy, though perhaps I have been setting
it out as a torture: a shock, an impalement, and so forth.
But finally, seeking reality is a joy because it is already all
around us; it is what we cannot help but find. Seeking
reality is a joy because we are ourselves real, and to affirm
reality is to affirm ourselves. The world, finally, is where we
frolic. One can truly play only if one can forget oneself;
self-loathing is the highest and deepest barrier to self-forgetting. Vice seduces us to self-forgetting but, finally, calls
us back into self-loathing. Transgression as sacrament,
however, gives us to forget ourselves, and allows us to play
in and with the world; it releases us from the tyranny of
our own judgments. It calls us to a love of the world and to
a love of each other: a sexual love, perhaps, and a sexual
play as a celebration of embodiment.

When we are seduced into self-forgetting, the first
thing we forget is our seriousness. Human beings, again,
may someday perish from a surfeit of seriousness, and no
event is more fearful than forgetting how to play. To play in
the world is to pay tribute to the world's reality, for to play,
too, is to be seduced by the real. There is no deeper form of
self-forgetting than to lose oneself in a game or in the creation of a work of art. And notice that these things require
stuff—we need swings, playing cards, canvas, and so forth.
Play is immersion in things, and, hence, is itself sacramental, or, rather, sacred. Even vice is play, or begins as
play, and that shows what is unsatisfactory about vice: It is
not carefree enough, is not playful enough, is enslaving. A
transgression that has ceased to be play has become a
vice, and is inimical to the life of the person whose vice it is.
All destruction and all creation are desirable if only they
can remain playful, for then can they lend us the joy of
self-forgetting. It would be sweet to become sugar; on the

other hand, sugar itself is sweet, and to experience its sweetness by taste is to experience the joy of self-forgetting. One does not need, hence, to become sugar as long as one is capable of enjoying the taste of sugar. But if one is perishing from a surfeit of sugar, becoming sugar may finally be the only way out.

For, finally, the only way out of vice is deeper into it; the only way out of the world is into the world entirely. The only "cure" for vice is the final seduction: an absolute allowance of the vice to be, which is an absolute allowance of myself to be vicious. To stop being an alcoholic, I need, finally, to dissolve into a puddle of alcohol: to acknowledge that I am, always was, and always will be an alcoholic: that my will is useless. That is, at this point I can no longer enjoy the taste of alcohol, and the only seduction that remains is oneness: I've got to become alcohol: to allow myself to be alcoholic. To do that is to expunge my will, not by an act of will but by an acknowledgment that my will has already been destroyed. To drink oneself into the depths of alcoholism is to engage in a sacrament until one dies or oneself becomes a sacrament. To have one's will *broken* is not precisely to be seduced, which is accompanied by the sensation of *letting one's will go*, but it is, nevertheless, a leaving behind of will. To be an alcoholic, then, is to be *broken*: to have one's will broken, like a wild horse whose wildness must be destroyed. And it is to be broken by the world, by reality, that is, by the sacred.

If that sounds painful, I'm here to tell you that it is, and excruciatingly so. But I am also here to report that there is the corresponding joy of self-forgetting, that having one's will broken is an invitation to play. That one affirms the world not by an act of will but because the world extorts affirmation from one—that is the greatest happiness I have known, or of which I take myself to be capable. Every aspect in which the real demands from us acknowledgment is an invitation to use the real to play; every self-forgetting is a letting-go of seriousness, an opportunity to dance. That is why the vices, finally, become sacraments: because they bring our seriousness near the surface, where it can be drawn off. They teach us the pleasure of letting go through the pain of holding on. They expunge our will by inflating our will to monstrous proportions. They allow us to let go by forcing us to let go.

7

Obscenity, Embodiment, Death

To experience ourselves as real is to experience ourselves as being situated within what is real. The experience of ourselves as real is, thus, an experience of finitude, of coming up against limits. We are without remainder of the order of things, that is, we are things. In that sense we are "one" with the world, and the enlightenment that has been sought in an identity of person and world is real enlightenment. But we are, as I have discussed, always in a particular situation; a human being is a certain real-world situation. The peculiar experience that reality offers us is the experience of ourselves as real, as belonging to the order of reality, and, at the same time, and inseparably, the experience of ourselves as particular, as situated within that order.

Whereas spirit stuff, mind stuff, text, ectoplasm is amorphous and without clear bounds, physical things are spatially and temporally finite. Thus, to experience ourselves as finite is to experience ourselves as real things in a real world. Our finitude is available to us in two directions: temporally and spatially. To experience ourselves as temporally finite is to experience ourselves as things that die. To experience ourselves as spatially finite is to experience ourselves as bodies.

It is not surprising, therefore, that a prodigious amount of human energy has been devoted to denying the reality of death, to promising an afterlife, and to denying our status as mere bodies, to making us out to be spirits and souls and texts. That is, the energy that is expended in denying reality is first trained on the reality of the self. And, of course, these two modes of denial (of our temporal and spatial limits) are connected: It is the soul that survives death, since the body's longevity is obviously limited. One would suppose from an examination of the history of religion and philosophy that it is ignominious to have limits. And certainly, death is often ignominious, a slow descent through pain and debility to extinction. For that reason, we praise death in battle or sudden heart attacks during sex ("in the saddie"). And one would suppose from Western intellectual history also that it is ignominious to be a hairy animal that craps and fucks.

Despite all appearances, we human beings never die, but persist in a purified state: Consider for a moment the monstrous self-mistrust and self-hatred that are exemplified in that familiar assertion. That we are not physical animals, that we do not die—such claims are obviously false; they are contradicted by what we all see is the case. Thus, I mistrust my seeing, even as what is expressed in these doctrines is my mistrust of my living. One must *hate oneself* so much for being a mortal animal that one can build an entire fictional universe, one that is ultimately incomprehensible, and actually come to believe that one lives *there* rather than *here*. And as Mark Twain pointed out in *Letters from the Earth*, what we seek in heaven is precisely what we would actually reject were it offered to us. If, for example, some angel were to appear and offer to relieve us of the burden of having sex (perhaps by genital mutilation), we would certainly refuse. We regard sex as perhaps the greatest human pleasure. But we carefully edit it out of heaven, where, as Twain says, people who hate music will choir and strum harps as they float around looking for something to do.

It would be comical, wouldn't it, to mount an *argument* that we are animals or that we are mortal. We spend all day, every day, in testimony to these facts; they are the facts that implicate us most intimately and inextricably;

they are our bounds, and we come up against them always. I am not prepared to *prove* that I am no immortal soul. The tiny operations of our will are, as I discussed in the last chapter, celebrated as a demonstration of our freedom from these bounds: That celebration is a forgetting of what we know most intimately. I *experience* the falsity of the claim that I am an immortal soul constantly by virtue of being alive. And I am, at times, well enough disposed toward my aliveness that I do not think it ignominious to be an animal. In fact, I find it rather fun, much of the time. Every attempt to deny or evade the most fundamental aspects of human existence testifies to the depth of sickness to which human beings can descend and to the resources at the disposal of human self-loathing.

To be a body is to be spatially limited, and this entails that we are of the nature of and embedded in the world. To be a thing that dies is to be temporally limited, to emerge out of and return to the earth. As these things establish our boundedness, they also establish our connections to what lies beyond our bounds. To experience one's limits is to experience what lies beyond one's limits as both genuinely other to and genuinely connected with oneself. And to acknowledge one's limits is to affirm oneself. Of course, to say that I am an immortal soul has the ring of an affirmation. But it says of me what cannot be true of things such as me and what denies the validity of my experience. It makes me as I experience myself unaccountable, arbitrary, bizarre. It flees my limits, and as it does so it flees what lies beyond my limits; my escape from myself can be accomplished only in an escape from the world and vice versa. There is a certain quixotic nobility in this quest, but one need hardly drive home its absolute futility. Every single authentic fact we experience must be falsified, distorted, destroyed, edited, reinterpreted as an emanation from or a message to spirit. The "soul" is a massive machine for the reprocessing of all experience into something false, miragelike, flimsy and wavering as a stage set.

I.

All obscenity is related to the salient signs of embodiment: Whatever bluntly asserts embodiment is transgressive. Being an animal body (a "bitch," say) *is* the obscene; it must be repressed. You may perhaps have wondered why certain words are "dangerous," since words seem to be merely innocent abstract objects that are incapable of inflicting any concrete damage. There are, however, certain words that one does not use in "polite" society or "mixed" company. These words ought not to be used around children, and ought not to be used by children, and cannot be used in public media such as television and "family" newspapers. All of this is an index of our hatred and fear of our own bodies; it is the human body that is, above all things, hedged about with taboos and weird magical beliefs. Every obscenity is a sign of procreation, ingestion, or excretion, the three most salient reminders that we are animal bodies: "fuck," "eat me," "shit," "cunt," "asshole," "schlong," to begin with. It is dangerous to teach children that they are animal bodies. It is dangerous to remind women, who, above all men, are supposed, in one zone of men's symbology, to be disembodied and spiritual, that they are animal bodies; they are too "delicate" for that. Women must be taught not to be bodies; they must be imaginatively "volatilized," or treated as pure spirits (at least for the time being!), precisely because we men find their reality as bodies too poignant to be easily borne. Women are ethereal, barely there at all (until the moment when their thereness is all-encompassing). Women must be protected from the bodies of men (and, of course, converting them into ectoplasm or text would provide an absolute protection), but, above all, they must be protected from their own bodies, and it is indelicate even to remind them that they are bodies.

Meantime, in another region of the imaginary women are supposed by men to lead a hidden, subterranean, massively embodied life that is, for men, the mystery *par excellence*—the life of menstruation, ovulation, pregnancy, childbirth, menopause, all of which comprise a relentless reminder of embodiment, and all of which are hedged around with ritual and taboo. It is precisely because women are imagined as so intensely embodied, and embodied in ways that men find so incomprehensible, that they must be made over again into pure souls, even if this, at its pathological extreme, involves literally killing them. The serial killer who attacks prostitutes is attacking them for their presence in their own bodies and for their presence to him as bodies; he is attacking embodiment: sex and the mysteries of the reproductive system. These beliefs can become so intense that the very notion that women have sex, much less enjoy it, becomes intolerable. That we purport to treat women—who, in Native American and other belief systems, are tied physically to the cycles of the moon and the tides—as more spiritual, that is, less physical, than men, who are gross and animalistic, is a bizarre and eloquent testimony to our horror of whatever is real. And whether we imagine women as less or more embodied than ourselves, our problematic relation to women's embodiment is an instrument of domination or negation.

The attempt, enforced in a thousand subtle ways, to remove obscene words from public discourse is a systematic attempt to forget the all-encompassing fact of embodiment. The acts themselves of fucking, jerking off, eating, pissing, shitting, and so forth are hedged around with ritual prohibitions. They are performed in special chambers in an elaborately mannered fashion. And they are, rather obscurely, associated with one another, so that one may eat in a suggestive manner, or eat off a nude person, or perform acts of excretion in association with the sex act. (Yeats: "But love has pitched his mansion in/The place of excrement."[1]) As the salient symptoms of animal embodiment, they are pushed beneath the surface of social life, so that you could almost go through your day thinking that you were the only one who did such things. Not only the acts, but even the signs for the acts, the words that pick out the acts, become transgressive. The obscene words are an eruption of the body into the aseptic realm of concepts, where everything is supposed to be safe and only slightly affecting. What in the world is the word "cocksucker," say, doing in this sweet little world of abstract concepts? Even its *sound* is invasive here; it is awfully percussive and Anglo-Saxon for the latinate world of general terms.

Thus, not only the acts themselves but the words for the acts and the concepts of the acts become means of transgression, that is, means of doing evil and of experiencing joy and release into the real. When a rapper or a comedian issues a stream of obscenity, he is not only being "earthy," as we revealingly say, but inviting us to enjoy our embodiment by violation of the taboos surrounding it. Or he is seducing us into reality by a transgression of the taboos surrounding *that*. For ultimately, it is reality that is taboo, so that every eruption of the real into the realm of concepts is "obscene." When seventeenth-century Dutch painters wanted to show the vanity of the world, thus assisting our ascent into the realm of spirit, they did it by painting fruit, sometimes fruit that had started to rot or was being eaten by insects. The insects and the rot were horrible enough, but it was the fruit that was "vain," that stubbornly clung to reality in a useless display of bodily integrity.

To repeat, though, the realm of spirit is a cheerless place, an awfully arid atmosphere for lush hairy tropical fuckers such as we. Every reminder of embodiment is at once a transgression, a seduction into sin, and a pure joy. Dance is loss in embodiment, and to dance to, say, Madonna's "erotic," or to some rapper hurling obscenities is joy indeed. And these are, in the sense developed earlier, also our truest moments, the moments in which we are most authentic. Taking a dump is, in this sense, a more authentic act than writing a book. To be lost in sex is to be lost in embodiment, woven into the world's web, situated. For that reason, sex is real and sex is joyful. Everything that is truly beautiful in this world is a reminder of embodiment and a symptom of joy taken in actuality. Hence, all real beauty is transgressive, is obscene. The attempts to purge beauty of obscenity—for example, the doctrines of the Neoplatonists or the paintings of Raphael—are always blank, empty. The female nude body is the paradigmatic beautiful object of Western art because Western culture hedges the female body around with taboos, and wants nothing more deeply than to violate those taboos, so that the nude female body is the most desirable thing there is (even, perhaps, for women); to be seduced by the nude female body is to be called into the real, into a perfect affirmation of one's own embodiment in the earth's body.

It is worth taking a moment to appreciate the virulence and the ridiculousness of the responses to the fact that embodiment is experienced as an obscenity. People have reared huge edifices of thought, from the Pythagoreans to the gospels to Hegel and beyond, to show the falsity of what everyone can see is obviously the case. That we are hairy things that shit and fuck is about as evident as anything can be, and it is evident to anyone. But despite all appearances, we are supposed to be immaterial souls inhabiting no particular place or taking up brief residence in a mammal. *Why* the soul resides in a mammal is thus the religiophilosophical mystery *par excellence*. In fact, this problem *is* the Western philosophical tradition, whereas it has usually not even been clearly formulated in non-Western traditions. In other words, the Western philosophical tradition is an attempt to grapple with obscenity, to remove it, censor it, deny it, repress it. Notice that the "mind/body" problem conditions the various treatments of ontology; the taxonomy of ontological theories—materialism, idealism, dualism—is articulated precisely out of responses to this problem. The place of God the Ghost in a physical universe is merely the same problem made grandiose. The debate between advocates of "free will" and determinism, the problem of evil, even esoteric modal logic issues such as the relativity of identity: All of them are motivated and sustained by the question of what in the world a mind is doing trapped in an animal's body. Or, to put it delicately, all these issues come down to one grand, overarching question: Why do I (the great philosopher) need to take a leak?

Even experiencing that as a problem, much less experiencing it as *the* problem, the problem within which one's tradition unfolds, is sick. People who cannot tolerate their own bodies are ill. In this sense, the Western tradition is an illness and a response to illness. One could, after all, easily imagine people who *enjoy* being bodies—perhaps you have even met such people, or perhaps you are yourself such a person. Everyone who is not maimed in the relevant respect, for example, has enjoyed an orgasm, a dance, a sport, a cuddle, a meal. Indeed, most folks enjoy such things quite frequently. But the intensity of this enjoyment seems, in the West, to be paid for in guilt, so that the more capable one is of enjoying the body, the more virulently must the body be rejected. In this sense, the history of asceticism is a tribute to the poignancy of bodily pleasure: The measures that must be taken to eliminate it are so extreme that the pleasures eliminated must be correspondingly compelling. Thus, asceticism is one long covert celebration of, or tribute to, the body. To castrate oneself in an ecstatic affirmation of God is to reveal just how much one's life is ruled by one's balls, so that any amelioration or mitigation is hopeless; elimination is the only option.

Dualism and idealism, which are intellectual asceticisms, imaginary mortifications of the flesh, thus testify always to the power of the body and the seductiveness of the pleasures of the body. The person who experiences himself as a mind, as ontologically distinct from his body, ought to be able simply to regard the body and the earth with amused indifference. Having risen above it all in a prospective construction, he ought to be able to rise above it all right in the present moment. But reality, we know, gives the soul no surcease. You are a mind now. But you are hungry now, horny now, in pain now, embedded in a situation that presents you with a myriad of dangers, promises, questions. When you consult your experience, the fact that you are a body is more obvious than that two plus two equals four. Thus, you must redouble your repression, you must truly take repression to heroic lengths, so as to deny all that is most obvious and believe what is obviously absurd.

Thus, the repression of the intellectual ascetic must be total; it is a systematic repression of *all* facts, because all facts must be reinterpreted as "spiritual." And, of course, various physical laws must be suspended, as, for example, the law of causation, which now proceeds from spirit to matter. When it reaches its height in idealism, this imaginary asceticism, having turned away from the world and into the spirit, now turns around in a rage and wreaks vengeance on the world. Here, the world itself is an outflowing of spirit; physical existence is an obscure reflection of the invisible. This is really an insane labyrinth, but all repression brings rage, and the rage of philosophers against the world is a rage that cannot be discharged by any actual act, that can only be discharged imaginatively. Idealism, thus, is an imaginary immolation of the world into spirit, and the symptom of a loathing for the world, and, in particular, a loathing of oneself as a body, so intense that it seeks to expunge all other impulses.

One odd feature of this repression and rage is that it is not particularized. No doubt, it first emerged in response to particular situations, particular bodily functions, particular environmental threats, particular frustrated desires, and so forth. But by the time it becomes a religion or a philosophical system, it has turned into a hatred of everything that exists, in virtue of its existence. Or rather, because hatred in the usual sense must tacitly acknowledge the existence of what is hated, it has turned into a sheer negation, a void or emptiness at a person's center that swallows up the world. Where the openness of the person to truth creates a space in which things are allowed to be, the void at the center of an idealist or an ascetic swallows all things, consigns them to oblivion. Not, to be sure, in actuality, where the like impulse expresses itself in making weapons or spewing toxic waste, but in imagination, where oblivion is relatively easy. Rather, all imagination calls thus to the real for its oblivion; all imagination is at heart an emptiness waiting for the real.

Thus, it is flight from body that makes the void, and the void imaginatively swallows all things. One odd feature of this is, as I say, its generality, so that the hatred of the world knows no limits or finds itself incapable of making exceptions. Imagine Kant saying to himself, All this that occurs in space and time and by causation is my prospective construction, but Juanita, she alone is real. Likewise, however, as Clement Rosset has very eloquently asserted, the joy of living, the affirmation of the real, becomes uncontrollably elaborated through all things, until we are in love with the world. Rosset writes:

The charm of autumn, for example, is related less to the fact that it is autumn than to the fact that it modifies the summer before, in turn, finding itself modified by winter. And its real "being" consists precisely in the modification that it brings about. But one can hardly imagine what would make up the charm of autumn "in its essence," as the disciple of Plato might want to imagine it. I would add that an autumn in its essence, no matter how one might represent it, primarily and especially would not be very "autumnal." This goes to show that the charm of existence, far from being appreciated in proportion to a problematic participation in eternity, is measured, on the contrary, in proportion to its distance from being as it is conceived by ontologists and metaphysicians—like autumn, which exists only if there is no "being" of autumn. . . . [J]oy is an unconditional rejoicing for and with respect to existence.[2]

Now, this passage speaks, first, about situation and the mistake involved in ontological decontextualization, so that to remove the limits imposed on a thing by its relations is also to remove that thing. But the unconditional rejoicing that is really the theme of Rosset's book is the counterpart to the complete condemnation of what is that necessarily arises as the Western tradition comes to grips with the body (so to speak). And as Rosset very rightly says, this rejoicing in existence seeks not to deny the tragic possibilities of existence but to rejoice in them as well as in life's pleasures. This is something that, in my best moments, I have actually experienced: *joy* in living in the world, though the world crushes me. If Kant had started with Juanita's reality, he could have found the whole world again in one perfect affirmation and have come to affirm it all. Or rather, he could have come not to regard all things as good, say, but to love all things, even those things he despised, even those things that endangered him or filled him with loathing.

Thus, our experience at each moment, by a perhaps small pleasure that it makes available to ourselves as bodies, is a call into every bit of the world. Once one starts to love one's body in the world and hence to love the world—that is, once one comes to love some particular situation in which one finds oneself (say, as one makes love)—one can be drawn into a love of things in general. Every joy that one finds in one's body or finds in the world for one's body is a road into sheer joy, sheer love of the real for its reality. And note, the very fact that we are animal bodies and spend more or less all day every day doing what animal bodies must do or like to do (breathing, for example) makes a love of the real available to us at all times. If we simply allow ourselves as bodies to experience what we are, as bodies, experiencing, we will be taken fully into situation and joy in situation.

That is why love of the real takes the form of posture, gesture, dance. One *opens oneself* as a body to music and to other bodies in dance, and thus brings oneself into affirmation. For we of the West, thinking ourselves toward affirmation is always dangerous, for thinking is precisely what seems to us to separate us from situation. But to make a gesture of openness to things, to open your arms in a preparation to embrace a lover, or the world as a lover—that is to find the joy of life. This is not a joy found only where there is pleasure. On the contrary, it is a joy at its most intense precisely within and throughout pain. But every pleasure of the body calls us into the possibility of this joy, makes us aware that it awaits us out there, in and as the world.

II.

Perhaps the most profound discussion of death in philosophy is found in Kierkegaard. He resists—or rather, ridicules—all attempts to conceptualize death, to treat it as an "issue" or a "question" to which a philosopher might seek an "answer." He writes:

> I know concerning [what it means to die] what people in general know about it; I know I shall die if I take a dose of sulfuric acid, and also if I drown myself, or go to sleep in an atmosphere of coal gas, and so forth. . . . I know the Stoics regarded suicide as a courageous deed, and that others consider it a cowardly act. . . . I know that the tragic hero dies in the fifth act of the drama, and that death here has an infinite significance in pathos; but that when a bartender dies, death does not have this significance. . . . I know furthermore what the clergy are accustomed to say on this subject, and I am familiar with the general run of themes treated at funerals.[3]

To know all of these general truths about death, however, is not to know about death. In fact, it is Kierkegaard's point that one piles up such general truths precisely in a (futile) flight from death: that the more general facts one knows about death, the less one knows death. He continues:

> I had become so learned and highfalutin that I had forgotten to understand what some time will happen to me as to every human being—sometime, nay, what am I saying: suppose death were so treacherous as to come tomorrow! Merely this one uncertainty, when it is to be understood and held fast by an existing individual, and hence enter into every thought . . . generates inconceivable difficulties.

An authentic encounter with or understanding of death, for Kierkegaard, is precisely a reminder that we are particular existing human beings and not "something in general." My death, which is moment by moment uncertain, *is* my temporal particularity, what distinguishes me from "World History," and if I hold it fast, death, which is moment by moment uncertain, whispers or howls to me of my particularity, calls me back to myself. *Your* death, the death of my "reader" might be for me something in general, but *my* death is *my* extinction: It cannot be *for me* something in general. As Kierkegaard says, perhaps for "systematic philosophers" their own death is "something in general," as it was for "the late Herr Soldin": "When he was about to get up in the morning he was not aware that he was dead." But I will not be present after my death to draw its lessons for systematic philosophy. I am always on *this* side of death, always, at every moment, confronting extinction as a wall, as something that cannot be traversed, as an absolute limit beyond limits.

As I say, the death of my reader might be for me something in general, an abstraction, because "the reader," like "the president" is some something in general. The death of "the president" is a *national* tragedy, which is to say that it is no one's tragedy in particular. The death of generalities like "the president" would always be a cause for celebration, were it not that generalities can never die. "The king is dead; long live the king." *Running* for President is a way of trying to *make oneself over* fantastically into a generality, and hence not to be subject to death any longer. The fact that this resistance to death turns out to be precisely a turning away from life is not even ironic. For anyone who experiences it as a tragedy for themselves, the death of the president is no longer the death of the president but the death of someone particular.

But of course, it is not only my own particularity that I find frustrating or intolerable but also precisely the particularity of people whom I love. For, to repeat, to experience love is to experience the loved one as utterly particular. And that experience is always dangerous; for one thing, it always threatens you by calling on you to affirm what you despise. The experience of love thus threatens to shatter your values or to turn you against your values. Thus, for example, someone you love can *get you to violate your principles*, and so forth: To commit yourself to love is to bring yourself into the threat of utter particularity, the threat of situation. This threat is brought home most forcefully when someone you love dies or is faced with death, because here one is reminded, again and again and inexorably, of the perfect particularity of the person whom one loves. Recently bereaved people find one thing more offensive than all others: the suggestion that the beloved could be *replaced* in their lives by someone who *fulfills the same function.* Death is always an invitation to and a reminder of the particularity of existence, which is precisely how Kierkegaard uses it in the quoted passage.

Nature is profligate. It expends a thousand seeds to produce a single viable tree. Individual human beings are, like the seeds of trees, extremely fragile. We "drop like flies," in huge battles or monsoons or in trivial little accidents or by the arbitrary actions of microbes or toxins. We, or some of us, place ultimate value on human lives; the world seems unimpressed by our valuations. It kills us one at a time or in groups, without any sign of regret. A momentary lapse in alertness, a nibble of *Bon Vivant* vichyssoise, and the world finds itself forced to make due without us.

The death of people I love yanks me into reality even as it attacks and destroys me. It leaves me defenseless, tenuous; it calls out of me a rage at the real that is an acknowledgment of its reality. When my brother died, as I have said, I wanted to *tear down* the world, and build it again on a revised basis. The experience of his death thus became, for me, the experience of the absoluteness of my limits. I could not, at first, come to grips with the finality of my brother's extinction, but I experienced the real as a bludgeon that threatened unconsciousness (hence also, and horrifyingly, as a seduction). The death of someone that one loves is capable of severing one's connection to reality, of driving one crazy. But even if it does that, it does it in virtue of creating an experience of the real that is absolutely poignant.

This reality is related to the violence of embodiment, and the violence by which we let go of embodiment into eroticism, obscenity, identification, oblivion, death. Bataille writes:

> In essence, the domain of eroticism is the domain of violence, of violation. But let us ponder on the transitions from discontinuity to continuity. . . . If we relate such transitions to our own experience, it is clear that there is most violence in the abrupt wrench out of discontinuity. The most violent thing of all for us is death which jerks us out of a tenacious obsession with the lastingness of our discontinuous being. (*Erotism*, 16)

The "abrupt wrench out of discontinuity" that is eroticism, seduction, death, is precisely what calls out our resistance, because it is precisely what we most desire. Thus, the death of another threatens us with our own ecstasy, with the moment in which our existence as discontinuous beings lapses.

And this is the structure of our contact with the real that, to one degree or another, informs all human emotional and intellectual history. That is, one experiences the reality of the real, the poignancy of the real, with ever-increasing intensity, and just where the poignancy is most intense (and the death of someone one loves is as intense a spot as any), one finds oneself faced with the necessity of repression. This, in turn, becomes generalized into a repression not only of the particular recalcitrant fact but of all recalcitrant facts and, finally, of all facts, in a maintenance of discontinuity. The degree to which philosophy has been created by death—for example, the degree to which our tradition reflects infant mortality or plague—has not been sufficiently appreciated. Philosophy in this sense is a repression of death, now generalized into a repression of life, for the very good reason that everything that lives dies. That is, philosophy is a compensation for death which itself kills.

The flight from the reality of death is testified to most eloquently in the unbelievable elaborateness of the strategies for its denial. Jean-Luc Nancy writes that "God has always signified, for as long as there has been a 'god,' that death *is not*; and God has always been that which infinitely overtakes death, withdrawing its prey from it in advance, conceding to it no more than the simulacrum of its mortal operation."[4] That the death of people one loves, or the prospect of it, is something one cannot face squarely—the history of philosophy and religion is as much a testimony to that as to anything. Philosophers and religionists are, perhaps, on the whole, unusually sensitive people, that is, people who are particularly vulnerable to the world. And when the world is experienced most acutely, especially in its Kali aspect as destroyer, killer, it must be retreated

from or escaped. Elaborate philosophical and religious systems are (this will be a familiar point by now) precisely
attempts to evade destruction. But, of course, this is a
strangely generalized response to the possibility of destruction; what threatens one with destruction is embedded in
the real, and the philosopher or religionist, hence, just to
be on the safe side (and in a structure of thought we have
just traversed), rejects reality lock, stock, and barrel. (Of
course, there are many other aspects of reality besides
destruction that are problematic. But leave these aside for
the moment.)

Now, as it were, we try to replace reality with the movie
set of a philosophical or religious "interpretation" or perhaps with a text or narrative. I don't know whether you
have ever actually been on a movie set (or, for that matter,
at Disney World) and tried to imagine yourself to be, say, in
space or in the Old West, but if you have, you may have
noticed how flimsy the set is as a replacement for the Old
West, how small it is in comparison with the Old West,
how *unrealistic* it is—finally, all things considered. One
could not, for example, come to *live* in a movie set for more
than a few moments without becoming aware that it was a
set one was inhabiting. In order to keep that fact out of
one's awareness, one would have to engage in an incredibly
intense process of self-deception, and even then one would
never be able to relax one's guard against reality.

It is likewise in the repression of the possibility of one's
own destruction, the intense imaginary preservation of
one's discontinuity, to which so much philosophy and religion are dedicated. The cognitive costs of such defenses
are astronomical, because finally the whole world must be
falsified in order to sustain this one belief in the face of
inexorable reality. And in the words of Chairman Mao,
"Repression breeds resistance." Note that this was said by
a master of political repression. When the reality of death is
excluded, evaded, explained away, it continually explodes
back into consciousness. People die. And though you think

they are on their way to a better place, you have an unaccountable grief for their absence from this one and an unaccountable fear of your own ascension. Thus, you might think of the history of philosophy and religion as a long fight against the reality of death. Death—in the form of particularity, subjectivity, defiance of orthodoxy (that is, in the form of sin and seduction into sin)—continually erupts into the machinery of repression, is continually beaten back, continually erupts again.

Notice that these things—particularity, subjectivity, defiance of orthodoxy—are associated, by Havel, for instance, precisely with life. That is, fleeing death is, precisely, death; fleeing death is dying. It is the world that kills. Or: life is fatal. In the words of Hank Williams: "I'll never get out of this world alive." So to evade death we flee precisely from the actual; to hold on to life we flee precisely from life. All of the energy and intelligence that has been focused on evading death has been calling us precisely out of life, that is, toward death. And notice that these evasions of death finally become celebrations of death, so that the evasion of death makes of death a siren's song. The taboo insists on its own transgression, records and enforces the possibility of transgression. For we are promised in death "eternal life," "eternal bliss," "paradise." Keep in mind that these very things *are death*. We seek to evade death by falsifying the reality of extinction, but our evasion becomes precisely a loving of death, which it must be, for it is a hatred of this world.

The hatred of death calls us to a blanket condemnation and repression of the world that kills. Here is a passage, however, from the *Chuang Tzu*, which shows how the affirmation of death can call us into a joy taken in the world:

Chuang Tzu's wife died. When Hui Tzu went to convey his condolences, he found Chuang Tzu sitting with his legs sprawled out, pounding on a tub and singing.

"You lived with her, she brought up your children and grew old," said Hui Tzu. "It should be enough simply not to weep at her death. But pounding on a tub and singing—this is going too far, isn't it?"

Chuang Tzu said, "You're wrong. When she first died, do you think I didn't grieve like anyone else? But I looked back to her beginning and the time before she was born. Not only the time before she was born but the time before she had a spirit. In the midst of the jumble of wonder and mystery a change took place and she had a spirit. Another change and she had a body. Another change and she was born. Now there's been another change and she's dead. It's just like the progression of the four seasons, spring summer, fall, winter.[5]

Notice that, as in Rosset and, in fact, in the commonplace manner of funeral treatments, life and death are connected here to the seasons as a way of emphasizing embeddedness in a mutable world. And notice, then ignore, the talk about spirit, which is, in the manner of the Taoist sage, tossed in with supreme casualness and which represents no particular philosophy of what a human being is. What is important in this passage is the joy—expressed in movement and noise making—that the sage takes in life, though life is fatal. In the context of ancient Chinese culture, where the rituals surrounding death were extremely elaborate, Chuang Tzu's manner of mourning is a pure transgression, an obscenity. Chuang Tzu's joy is not happiness that his wife has died; he sorrows for the loss of a person he loves. But in his allowance of himself to mourn, precisely there, he finds a letting-go into affirmation. In letting himself be bereft, he unaccountably feels a joy that is total welling up within him. Pain and death, no less than the pleasures of the body, can call us into a joy at living, which is a measure both of human resilience and human perversity.

We are built, I suppose, so as to fear death and to want to preserve ourselves. As is usual with people, of course, this basic animal impulse gets twisted and elaborated into an object of labyrinthine complexity by consciousness. But our hatred and fear of death is, of course, natural; it is something we see in all animals or, indeed, as I have said, in all things that remain in existence, in all things that resist in any degree being pulverized. So our hatred of death shows how much, in fact, we really do love life. Our hatred of death, finally, is an affirmation of life. Even the promise of a paradisiacal afterlife shows—doesn't it?—that we would not yet be weary of life if life did less to make us weary.

Perhaps I have not yet emphasized this sufficiently, but I do believe that, just as all affirmation of the world is somehow stunted and incomplete, all of our negation of the world is partly false, or mere bluster in the face of the actual. When you get down to it, everyone who is not right now committing suicide still finds within herself a love of the world sufficient unto this day. Perhaps, on the whole, we love the world and our lives in the world more than we hate them, for even our hatred of the world is, finally, a twisted turning toward life, a yearning for life. The life we yearn for has, indeed, been expurgated, but what has been purged are (among other things) those very things that threaten our lives: evil persons, famines, plagues, predators, and so forth. When heaven includes feasts and beautiful serving girls, as in Islam, no man who loves life would be too averse to seeing it made eternal.

So our hatred of death expresses or emerges out of the life within us. Love is affirmation, and the death of someone we love is bereavement: Loss of the actuality of the beloved is the loss of love, so that love wants life, and hence rejects death. Love is also, however, a seduction into continuity. Death is, of course, one of the fundamental features of life: Without death there *can be* no life, for life requires spatial and temporal situatedness. Without continuity there can be no discontinuity; one's discontinuity is a continual seduction. Life is always, in that sense, particular and vulnerable or wounded; it is an opening. There can be no *awareness* of being alive without a concomitant vulnerability to the world, which is an always present reminder of situation. That, ultimately, is why a repression of death or of sex must become a repression of reality as a whole and why also an affirmation of death or of sex must become an affirmation of reality as a whole: because though the world only occasionally damages or kills us or brings us ecstasy, it does so at times of its, not our, choosing, so that there is no surcease whatever from our vulnerability.

Life without death is a sort of lingering, an amorphous nonexistence, an ectoplasmic drift over a ghostly environment. Here we revisit the "will to power." Like the desire for power over oneself and over others, the desire to evade death emerges from the directionality of life: life's momentum. But the desire to evade death, like the desire for power over oneself and others (Nietzsche, by the way, contemplated *replacing* the former with the latter in the theory of evolution) can turn against life. When the desire to evade death becomes a monomania, when we live lives devoted to the evasion of death, the life within us has become hostile to itself and its situation. We can see this perfectly clearly in, say, cases of hypochondria or in the case of Howard Hughes retiring into a hermetically sealed bubble to avoid microbes—he might as well already have been dead as try that hard to stay alive. To try to render oneself *invulnerable* to death—this is always to turn toward death itself, either by imaginatively repressing the world, as in idealism or in the promise of an afterlife, or by taking steps that actually lead to mortification of the body. The expunging of death increases its seductive power. The Taoists who sought the elixir of immortality died of their own prescriptions.

Thus, the hatred of death, which, to repeat, expresses life, becomes morbid, becomes itself a disease of which it is possible to perish. Life then calls us toward death: slowly, inexorably, and hatefully. It is possible to hear, in religions' claims to afterlife or in the claims of philosophical systems to comprehension, a love of life to which life itself has become hateful or intolerable. One learns to hate one's aliveness because it leads to death, even as one could not possibly hate death without loving life in the first place. Finally, as an expression of one's hatred of death, one "kills oneself," either by becoming a sort of human system or machine, as Kant, or by slitting one's wrists.

Then the turn back into life takes this form: *dare* death, *defy* death, live each moment as if it were one's last, and so forth. This is as if to really love life one would have to *seek* death (or rather, simulate death) by skydiving or bungee jumping or whatever. But this is a perfectly comprehensible response to a love of life so intense that it can no longer risk life, for fear of death. Here, risk, or even simulated risk, becomes affirmation, a turning back into actuality, and death becomes something that we must accept, if we are to accept life. Now, I am not suggesting, for instance, that the proper response to the death of someone one loves is immediate acceptance; that would be impossible even if it were desirable. What I am suggesting, rather, is that being overwhelmed by rage and sadness displays our utter embeddedness in the real, and this can lead finally into and beyond acceptance, as it does for Chuang Tzu. To repeat, when this experience of being overwhelmed reaches a fevered pitch, it will turn us away from the world as a whole as a world that kills what and whom we love. But if we were to have the courage and the vulnerability to remain within the rage and sadness, to allow ourselves to be sad and enraged, even enraged precisely at the universe, then we would have retained our love. Death calls us, like all seduction, precisely, back into reality, shows us the reality of ourselves and, beyond any shadow of doubt, the reality, now passed, of those whom, as we put it, we have lost.

Here, as elsewhere, concepts are flight, or it might even be true to say, as I have already said, that concepts are death: There are no general truths, only particular situations (that is itself a general truth). The structure of evasion embodied in the process of producing concepts and arguments is never more obvious than when it comes to death. I write about death as a conceptual problem in order to evade the intolerable fact that I myself am at every moment subject to death. But my "conceptualizing" of death is itself a dying or an imagination of dying, so that, in imagination, I shuffle off this mortal coil even as I philosophically discuss death. I want to *master* death by comprehension, but, of course, all the time death is calling precisely *me*. Our mastery of ourselves, to repeat an observation of a previous chapter, is itself performed at the expense of own lives and integrity; when I am mastering myself, I am, first, divided against myself into master and slave, and I am, second, using the life of the slave, that is, my own life, to feed the life of the master, that is, my own life. I am thus the parasite of myself.

But now, when I seek to *understand* death philosophically or psychologically or physiologically, I am seeking to master myself insofar as I am a thing that dies; or rather, I am seeking to master my own death, or to continue living. Thus, I kill myself precisely as an expression of the life within me; fear of death drives me precisely toward death, until death itself becomes a seduction into the real. Death, in this sense, can itself become a joy, or, at any rate, a solace. The death of ourselves as bodies saves us from a "fate worse than death," that is, becoming concepts, souls, or narratives. The "philosophical discussion of death," the mastery over death which we seek by concepts, is an attempt to render *ourselves* concepts, so that we are too abstract to perish. To allow myself to experience myself as a thing that dies is an allowance of myself to be a real thing, and, hence, is a seduction into actuality. Our own deaths are always *out there*, at the bound, beckoning us into actuality and then out of actuality. But even this destruction of the self, the absolute extinction of the person from the actual, is itself refreshingly actual, in that it is concrete, particular; it is destruction to all pretension of rendering the self an abstract object. My death really is, hence, my salvation: Death makes me something real, and as long as I can be true to my death, I can be true to myself and true to the world that kills me.

NOTES

1. The Shock of the Real

1. George Santayana, *Scepticism and Animal Faith* (New York: Dover, 1955 [1923]), 142.

2. Friedrich Nietzsche, *The Gay Science*, trans. Walter Kaufmann (New York: Vintage, 1974), 282–83.

3. Richard Rorty, "Philosophy as a Kind of Writing," *Consequences of Pragmatism* (Minneapolis: University of Minnesota Press, 1982), 100.

4. Henry David Thoreau, *A Week on the Concord and Merrimack Rivers*, reprinted in *Thoreau* (New York: Library of America, 1985), 233.

5. "The Recorded Conversations of Zen Master I-Hsuan," in *A Sourcebook in Chinese Philosophy*, ed. Wing-tsit Chan (Princeton: Princeton University Press, 1963), 446. I have adapted the translation.

6. Quoted in Shin'ichi Hisamatsu, *Zen and the Fine Arts*, trans. Gishiu Tokinsa (New York: Kodansha, 1971), 20.

7. *The Complete Works of Chuang Tzu*, trans. Burton Watson (New York: Columbia University Press, 1968), 240.

8. Lao Tzu, *Tao Te Ching*, trans. Stephen Mitchell (New York: Harper and Row, 1988), chap. 38.

9. Thich Nhat Hanh, *The Miracle of Mindfulness* (Boston: Beacon Press, 1987), 24.

10. *The Platform Sutra of the Sixth Patriarch*, trans. Philip B. Yampolsky (New York: Columbia University Press, 1967), 161.

11. D. T. Suzuki, *The Sense of Zen* (Garden City, NY: Doubleday Anchor, 1956), 11.

12. Ibid., 132.

13. Ibid., 113.

14. Nietzsche, *The Gay Science*, section 341.

15. Nietzsche, *Thus Spoke Zarathustra* (New York: Vintage, 1978), 13.

2. Truth, Home, Situation

1. Wendell Berry, *Remembering* (San Francisco: North Point Press, 1988), 65.

2. George Santayana, *The Life of Reason* (New York: Scribner's, 1954), 19.

3. Richard Wilbur, "Epistemology," *The Poems of Richard Wilbur* (New York: Harcourt, Brace and World, n.d.), 121.

4. Martin Heidegger, "On the Essence of Truth," trans. John Sallis, in *Basic Writings* (New York: Harper and Row, 1977), 124.

3. Authenticity, Affirmation, Love

1. Georges Bataille, *Guilty*, trans. Bruce Boone (San Francisco: City Lights, 1988 [1961]), 20.

2. Mark Twain, "On the Decay of the Art of Lying," in *Collected Tales, Sketches, Speeches, and Essays: 1852–1890* (New York: Library of America: 1992), 825.

3. Plato, *Symposium*, trans. Michael Joyce, in *Plato: Collected Dialogues* (Princeton: Princeton University Press, 1961), 562–563.

4. Nietzsche, *Beyond Good and Evil*, trans. Walter Kaufmann (New York: Vintage, 1966), 90.

5. Nietzsche, *Thus Spoke Zarathustra*, trans. Walter Kaufmann (New York; Penguin, 1978), 65.

4. Anarchy, Particularity, Reality

1. Henry David Thoreau, *A Week on the Concord and Merrimack Rivers*, in *Thoreau* (New York: Library of America, 1985), 104.

2. *Thus Spoke Zarathustra*, 49.

3. Vaclav Havel, "Politics and Conscience," in *Living in Truth* (Boston: Faber and Faber, 1986), 143. Further references to this volume will appear in the text by page number.

4. G.W.F. Hegel, *Philosophy of Right*, trans. T. M. Knox (Oxford: Clarendon Press, 1942), 288.

5. Søren Kierkegaard, *Concluding Unscientific Postscript*, trans. David F. Swenson and Walter Lowrie (Princeton: Princeton University Press, 1968), 169.

6. This point is beautifully developed by Miroslav Kusy, who refers to what Havel terms the post-totalitarian system as "real socialism": "In its entire spirit and thrust, real socialism is an ideology *als ob*, an ideology of *as if*: those who preach it behave *as if* the ideological kingdom of real socialism existed in 'what we have now,' *as if* they had, in all earnestness, convinced the nation of its existence; the nation behaves *as if* it believed it" ("Chartism and 'Real Socialism'," *The Power of the Powerless*, ed. John Keane [Armonk, NY: M. E. Sharpe, 1985], 164). Interestingly, Kusy has serious misgivings about the "existential" solution that Havel adopts.

7. "L'Anarchisme et les syndicats ouvriers," in *Les Temps Nouveaux*, Nov. 1895. Quoted in James Joll, *The Anarchists* (London: Methuen, 1979), 181.

8. Emma Goldman, *Anarchism* (New York: Dover, 1969), 43.

5. Power, Openness, Earth

1. Thoreau, *Walden*, reprinted in *Thoreau* (New York: Library of America, 1985), 328.

2. John (Fire) Lame Deer and Richard Erdoes, *Lame Deer Seeker of Visions* (New York: Simon and Schuster, 1994 [1972]), 121.

3. *The Sacred Pipe: Black Elk's Account of the Seven Rites of the Oglala Sioux*, recorded and edited by Joseph Epes Brown (Norman: University of Oklahoma Press, 1953), 19–20.

4. Ed McGaa, Eagle Man, *Mother Earth Spirituality* (San Francisco: Harper, 1990), 62.

5. Thomas Mails in dialogue with Fools Crow, *Fools Crow: Wisdom and Power* (Tulsa: Council Oak Books, 1991), 113.

6. Seduction, Transgression, Addiction

1. Georges Bataille, *Erotism* (San Francisco: City Lights, 1986 [1957]), 38–39.

2. Heinrich Zimmer, *Philosophies of India*, ed. Joseph Campbell (New York: Meridian, 1956), 575.

3. *The Gospel of Sri Ramakrishna*, quoted in Zimmer, *Philosophies of India*, 563.

4. Chogyam Trungpa, *Journey without Goal: The Tantric Wisdom of the Buddha* (Boston: Shambhala, 1985), 44.

5. Ibid., 135.

6. Quoted in Indra Sinha, *The Great Book of Tantra* (Rochester, VT: Destiny Books, 1993), 113.

7. Quoted in Omar V. Garrison, *Tantra: The Yoga of Sex* (New York: Harmony Books, 1964), 40.

8. Quoted in Sinha, *Great Book of Tantra*, 139.

9. Quoted in Garrison, *Tantra: The Yoga of Sex*, 98.

10. Barbara Tedlock, "The Clown's Way," in *Teachings from the American Earth: Indian Religion and Philosophy* (New York: Liveright, 1992), 106.

7. Obscenity, Embodiment, Death

1. W. B. Yeats, "Crazy Jane Talks with the Bishop," widely anthologized.

2. Clement Rosset, *Joyful Cruelty*, trans. David F. Bell (New York, Oxford University Press, 1993), 13, 15.

3. Søren Kierkegaard, *Concluding Unscientific Postscript*, trans. David F. Swenson and Walter Lowrie (Princeton: Princeton University Press, 1941), 146, 147. The quotes that follow are from the next couple of pages of my tattered edition. Memo to PUP: please reprint.

4. Jean-Luc Nancy, *The Birth to Presence* (Stanford, CA: Stanford University Press, 1993), 51.

5. *The Complete Works of Chuang Tzu*, 191–192.

INDEX